VOYAGE OF THE *SUZY WONG*

VOYAGE OF THE SUZY WONG

Paul Cardoza, Steve Jackson, George Todd, and Walter Banks
As told to Jonathan Lewis

WINDY CITY
PUBLISHERS

CHICAGO

Voyage of the Suzy Wong

Windy City Publishers
2118 Plum Grove Road, #349
Rolling Meadows, IL 60008
www.windycitypublishers.com

Published in the United States of America

First Edition: 2014

ISBN:
978-1-935766-78-0

Library of Congress Control Number:
2013934406

DEDICATION

SUZY
WONG

Crew members Paul Cardoza, Steve Jackson, George Todd, and Walter Banks dedicate their book to that lovely lady, the *Suzy Wong*, the handsome Sparkman & Stephens yawl that brought them safely home from Hong Kong to the shores of America, half a world away and half a century ago.

ACKNOWLEDGMENTS

The crew of the *Suzy Wong* wishes to thank: Steve Jackson for his efforts in putting the story of our voyage in book form; Paul Cardoza for initiating the project with his family memoirs; George Todd for having the inspiration to embark on the trip in the first place; and Walter Banks for navigating our boat safely home to America.

The crew would like to acknowledge Jonathan Lewis for crafting selected elements of our story into a captivating read.

We owe special thanks to Tony and John Cardoza, Elana Jackson, Ruth Jackson, and Helen Magid for their painstaking work editing the final text. We would also like to recognize Jeremy Pane and Bill Groetzinger for their assistance with publishing and graphic issues.

We are grateful to Windy City Publishers for their advice and direction throughout the publishing process.

Finally, we wish to impart courage to the future generations of our families and sailors. Having experienced this amazing voyage, we have learned that summoning the courage to follow one's dream is perhaps the most important accomplishment of a lifetime. We hope our readers will enjoy "coming aboard" the *Suzy Wong*.

TABLE OF CONTENTS

THE VOYAGE OF

PORTS OF CALL TRAVELED...

HONG KONG, CHINA	TRINCOMALEE, CEYLON
MANILA, PHILIPPINES	RAF GAN, MALDIVES
TRUMPITAO PT, PHILIPPINES	VICTORIA, SEYCHELLES
PALAWAN, PHILIPPINES	ADEN, YEMEN
JESSELTON, NORTH BORNEO	PORT SUDAN, SUDAN
BRUNEI, NORTH BORNEO	PORT SUEZ, EGYPT
SINGAPORE, MALAYSIA	PORT SAID, EGYPT
PENANG, MALAYSIA	BEIRUT, LEBANON
NICOBAR ISLANDS, INDIA	TOBRUK, LIBYA

THE *SUZY WONG*

...BY THE *SUZY WONG*, 1960–1961

PROLOGUE

A GRAND ADVENTURE

The idea for the voyage of the *Suzy Wong* was born in a bar in the Philippines late one night in May of 1959. In the sober light of the next day, it still seemed like a good idea. The crew of four former American servicemen—Steve Jackson, Paul Cardoza, George Todd, and Walter Banks—came together to put their plan in motion to build a boat in Hong Kong and sail it westward to America with the simple goal of seeing as much of the world as they could.

They had little sailing experience. In fact, one of them had never been on a sailboat! They knew the journey would be challenging, but they felt their combined military experience and individual skill sets would see them through any trouble they might encounter.

They bought plans for a forty-one-foot yawl and, over the course of many months, all four men helped in its construction. While living in Hong Kong, one of the crew had a chance meeting with a world-famous movie star, William Holden, who was then filming *The World of Suzie Wong*. That meeting led the crew to name their boat after the movie. This, in turn, led them to a publicist who used the voyage as a way to promote the movie and generate a little red-carpet treatment for the crew.

As if this journey wasn't sufficiently daunting, the four dismissed much of the advice offered by experienced sailors in favor of what felt right to them. They resolutely ignored the universal recommendation, "Do not bring a dog!" They did. They had fallen in love with a puppy in Hong Kong, so what else could they do?

These intrepid sailors (and one charming dog) would get to see far more of the world than most men their age see in a lifetime. They were about to embark upon their very own grand adventure.

Chapter 1

George and Steve

Like most Americans of their generation, George Todd and Steve Jackson had never traveled outside the United States before beginning their military service. In the late 1950s, international travel for personal pleasure was in its infancy and centered on the wealthy "jet setters." Most Americans back then preferred to stay in America. If sent abroad for military service, they would return back home as soon as they could.

George and Steve were different. These two met in Manila, in the Philippines, where both were assigned to the US Naval Base at Sangley Point. George Todd was the first to arrive in 1957 at the age of twenty-five. He was a philosophy graduate with a Quaker education from Haverford College in Pennsylvania, and then, fresh out of Pensacola Flight School, he became a lieutenant in the United States Navy. His new job as air transportation coordinating officer was a high-octane high-level position with great responsibilities.

George was a good-looking naval officer with a zest for life. He was quick-witted and could spin a good tale. Whether or not the stories he told were factual was beside the point. He was collecting life experiences, which included exploring different parts of the island of Luzon in the Philippines. One popular destination was the Thousand Islands at the south end of Lingayen Gulf, where the Allies had landed in 1945. Here he and a few of his buddies would explore the coral islands that dotted the bay using a banca boat, a Philippine boat having a canoe-like hull with an outrigger for stability.

Getting to the Thousand Islands was an experience in itself. The roads passed through endless stretches of jungle, with small villages here and there. Locals used the streets as their front yards, where children played and dogs, pigs, and chickens mingled about. Drivers had to navigate carefully to avoid hitting the living obstacles. To keep the villages safe, "sleeping policemen" (better known as speed bumps) were placed every fifty yards or so. Hitting one of those bumps at any reasonable speed sent the car's occupants flying to the ceiling.

George was assigned to replace his lieutenant commander, who was finishing his last duty station before retirement. The commander was a big, tough guy who hated Filipinos. His xenophobic chauvinism trumpeted trouble to the natives in the department. He even bullied fellow Americans into showing subservience. Everyone tiptoed around him. George got the message pretty quickly that, as the ignorant young upstart on base, he had better keep a low profile until it was time for his superior officer to depart.

On his first morning in charge, George called the guys together and made a little speech: "You all know that I don't know anything. So everyone who touches any piece of paper in this office will sign and date it. If I ever hang, you're going to hang sooner and higher." The response was, without reservation, "Yes, sir!" After that friendly greeting, he reassigned a Filipino to the chief's position and made other such reassignments from American to Filipino. Eventually, everyone breathed easier because they felt that finally this office of sixty-five men had a chance of functioning better than it ever had before.

Steve Jackson arrived in Manila a short time later. Steve was a graduate of Yale University, where he majored in industrial engineering and was an undefeated champion wrestler in his senior year. At Yale he enrolled in the ROTC program and graduated in 1957 as a second lieutenant in the United States Army.

After Signal Corps training at Ft. Monmouth, New Jersey, Steve and 250 of his classmates awaited their first duty assignments. As the last man to receive his orders, Steve found himself assigned to the Joint Army, Navy, and Air Force Frequency Allocation Board at Sangley Point in the Philippines. Everyone else was sent to Fort Huachuca, Arizona, Fort Bragg, North Carolina, or Korea. As the odd man out, Steve would be the lone army officer on the navy base at Sangley Point, serving as army liaison for the Signal Corps.

Steve was always ready to accept a challenge, and sometimes this willingness had as much to do with a certain naïveté as it was a spirit of adventure. In any case, he found himself in a distant land with all new people surrounding him and a whole new world to explore—the island of Luzon. Being the only army man on base, he had no obligation to carry out watch duty. His weekends were his to enjoy. Every now and then he wondered how his other Signal Corp buddies were faring, but, quite honestly, he was having too much fun to care.

Steve took flying lessons with a Filipino pilot he met by the name of Ray Santos, who had built himself a small Piper Cub-type airplane that he flew out of Manila International Airport. Aboard the plane, Steve had the entire island to discover, from Baguio in the north to the Mayon Volcano in the south. He thrilled at flying above the jungle treetops and over the rice terraces. What a splendid way to view his new territory!

The plane had no radio. Steve was partly color-blind and had trouble seeing the colored light signals that were used to guide pilots on take-off and landing. Often as his light plane was lifting easily into the air, a large four-engine commercial plane would be taking off directly underneath him. Despite some anxiety-ridden take-offs and landings at the international airport, every other aspect of flying was a joy for him.

Steve's commanding officer at Sangley, Commander Ellis Skidmore, had commissioned a boat to be built in Hong Kong in early 1959. The two men had become friendly, so when the thirty-seven-foot sloop named the *Ping Po* was ready, Skidmore asked Jackson to be part of his crew on its inaugural voyage from Hong Kong back to the Philippines. It didn't take Skidmore much effort to convince a willing Steve to join his crew on the *Ping Po* for Steve's first blue-water sailing experience.

The US Consulate in Hong Kong tried to cancel the trip when they learned that all of Skidmore's crew had high-level security clearances. They considered it unwise to expose the commander and his crew to possible capture by the navy of Communist China. This was, after all, during China's Great Leap Forward when Cold War tensions were high. But Commander Skidmore had permission from the military and the US Embassy in Manila, so they carefully avoided any contact with the US Consulate in Hong Kong and made a hasty departure the next day.

The first day of their voyage, seawater backed up into the engine through the exhaust pipe, making the engine inoperable. Over the next three days, the South China Sea went uncharacteristically flat, leaving Commander Skidmore and his crew dangerously close to Red China and drifting toward shore with the current. Steve was beginning to imagine what it would be like to spend the next several years in a Chinese prison. He was also aware of boats being seized by pirates in these waters—all very unsettling thoughts. Then, in a heroic effort, they managed to dismantle the engine, clear the saltwater from the pistons, reset the timing, and get the engine going again! In the last several hours of the voyage to Sangley Point, both wind for the sails and fuel for the engine ran out, leaving the *Ping Po* becalmed within eyesight of the pier where well-wishers waited patiently for the boat to dock.

Steve's first blue-water sail aboard *Ping Po*;
Sangley Point, Philippines

While this was Steve's first ocean voyage, he was not exactly a novice sailor. At age ten he had built a 2 x 3-foot boat of his own design (which promptly sank upon launching). He continued to build boats that were better in design and function and sail them on the waters of Lake Waccabuc in upstate New York. He became quite handy at maneuvering his homemade crafts around this small lake and forged a lasting fascination with boats. Now, having taken this weeklong voyage on the *Ping Po*, he had the appetite for an even grander adventure.

CHAPTER 2

BILLETING IN MANILA

Not long after his arrival in the Philippines, Steve began searching for accommodations in Manila. Barrack facilities were in short supply with the revolving door of military men coming and going throughout the year, so officers were commonly rotated off the base and into local housing. George was looking for another housemate and found Steve just at the moment when Steve needed to make other living arrangements.

George was living a comfortable life near Manila in Mandaluyong. Along with another Sangley officer, Dave Kenny, he was renting a house off base, the kind often referred to as a "snake ranch" because of all the single guys roaming around. This one had two guys living a luxurious life with a cook, a houseboy, a dog, and a monkey. Steve liked what he saw of the small house, felt comfortable with both George and Dave, and quickly agreed to become the third officer in residence.

Manila seemed like the lap of luxury to these three Americans. The weather was tropical and lovely, and the social scene was hospitable and welcoming to young servicemen in uniform. The girls were plentiful and spectacularly beautiful. There were the stewardesses who flew in and out of Manila on multiple airlines, the unmarried civilian ladies, and then there were the professional ladies of the night!

In the street outside their snake ranch they could hear the sounds of hawkers selling goods. One popular item was the Filipino balut, a ready-to-hatch duck embryo which could be boiled and eaten from the shell. Monkeys, dogs, and birds could be bought on the spot if you wanted a pet. The smell of cooking and warm tropical flowers was always in the air. To a Filipino, this was the familiar smell of home. To a foreigner, it was a reminder that you were in an exciting, new environment.

There were many economic opportunities around the base in Manila, some shadier than others. The United States issued a form of currency known as Military Payment Certificates, or MPCs, which were as good as dollars wherever they were officially recognized. Just like dollars, they were frequently used and abused by persons for whom they were not intended. Whenever the MPC activity got out of control, the United States declared them worthless and reissued a new series of certificates.

This sudden switch of currency would happen without warning one day in a big city base like Manila, for instance, but not in Tokyo until a short time later. With the help of stewardess "mules," enterprising individuals exploited this small window of opportunity to ferry the leftover, now defunct, MPCs from the Philippines to Japan, where they still had value. People in Tokyo hastily converted these certificates into dollars or yen just before the ax fell there as well. George narrowly escaped being convicted of this illegal activity when a stewardess friend handed him a bag of money and an address for delivery. He was called in and had to answer charges of involvement in the MPC racket. Fortunately for George, he was innocent and cleared of all charges.

Both George and Steve did become entrepreneurial by purchasing Philippine Long Distance Telephone stock in New York City and selling it in Manila for what turned out to be a handsome profit, taking legal advantage of the locally controlled currency.

Life in Manila often felt like a vacation for George and Steve. Since the United States was not at war, their duties were light and these two officers had plenty of free time to enjoy life in the Philippines. Some of that leisure time was spent in a local bar near their home where every couple of nights they would hang out to chat up the local lovelies and talk about their experiences.

Steve and George on weekend snorkel adventure; Philippines

It was on one such night (in May of 1959) that Steve shared with George tales of his sailing trip with Commander Skidmore aboard the *Ping Po* from Hong Kong to Manila. George remarked, "Let's build a boat and sail home!" Steve gave this idea careful consideration for all of about fifteen seconds before replying, "Sounds like a good idea, George. Let's do it!" Had they been a little older, their exciting idea might have run aground on more mature sensibilities, but George and Steve were young and spontaneous. To sail a boat halfway around the world seemed like a boy's fantasy for adventure. They didn't have a clue how hard it would actually be.

The next morning the idea still sounded great and planning started almost immediately. They began thinking of ways a boat could be built or bought. Hong Kong was certainly the place to start looking, especially following Commander Skidmore's experience. Money was also a concern, but living in Manila would be an advantage because household belongings, particularly cars, turned a handsome profit on the local market. George had brought a Cadillac to the Philippines, while Steve brought a Volkswagon. Both cars, when sold, would bring double their US value. They also figured that being in the navy would serve them well for gathering such things as nautical charts, navigational instruments, and seafaring knowledge. Excitement mounted as their plan grew from a crazy idea into a real plan of action and adventure.

On June 24, 1959, soon after considering the idea of the voyage, Steve wrote a letter to his parents to give them the news that he was about to embark on a trip that might strike them as crazy:

> This is the kind of experience that most people only dream about. At some point in one's life, such an opportunity will present itself. It is my contention that too many people let their dreams vanish—next year it is often too late. Right now I'm single, have the time, and can swing the trip. I would hate to look back in ten years with regret at having missed this trip of a lifetime.

Steve came by his adventurous spirit naturally. Both of his parents were airplane pilots in the early 1930s when flying was a hobby among the gentry. They had met in 1932 while participating in an air derby to Miami, flying open-cockpit planes equipped with only a compass, oil gauge, and altimeter. Having themselves rebelled against parental authority, Steve's mother and father knew they could hardly discourage their son with regard to his bold adventure. Realistically, there wasn't much they could do to influence their son, who was half a world away and independent in every sense of the word.

Once George's tour of duty ended, he decided to travel home to Troy, New York, to visit his elderly mother prior to embarking on the sailing adventure. As a courtesy, George promised to visit Steve's parents, Robert and Laura Jackson, in South Salem, New York, to tell them personally about their son's plan to sail to America from Hong Kong. George liked to spin a good yarn, so he wasn't above exaggerating the facts to make the story more interesting. He told Steve's parents that their son would be safe sailing with an expert seaman such as himself. In truth, George knew next to nothing about sailing and far less than Steve, who had spent summers sailing on Lake Waccabuc and, of course, a week on the *Ping Po*.

CHAPTER 3

THE SEARCH FOR A BUILDER BEGINS

George knew that Commander Skidmore's boat had been built in Hong Kong, so the search began there. Being the transportation officer at Sangley Point Naval Station, George had easy access to Hong Kong—a relatively short flight from Manila. He made several reconnaissance trips there to identify a boat and builder. Because of Commander Skidmore he knew of the Wing on Shing and Choi Lee shipyards, but he came away feeling confused and skeptical that he could have a boat built in a Chinese shipyard. Then George met Bob Newton and everything changed.

Bob Newton had begun developing his financial interests in Hong Kong during the maelstrom of political, social, and economic upheaval in China and the mass refugee exodus from the mainland. While he was not a longtime boat builder, he was a mature, savvy American businessman established in Kowloon, Hong Kong, and the owner of a Bireley's Orange bottling facility. Newton was developing a separate boat building business in Junk Bay called American Marine Limited. With his entrepreneurial spirit, he seemed the perfect person to help George turn his dream into a reality.

At the time, American Marine Limited was building a sailboat for Swedish film actor Max von Sydow following a design by the world's finest sailboat designer, Sparkman & Stephens. Newton explained to George how his company could easily build a replica of the von Sydow boat. They already had the plans, molds, and recent construction experience, which would keep costs down. Building a replica of von Sydow's boat would also allow George and Steve a good head start with their vessel, as the boatyard wouldn't be starting from scratch.

George contacted Max von Sydow and found him to be an approachable and agreeable person. The actor confirmed that he was happy with the progress being made on his boat and that it was, indeed, going to be an excellent sailboat. A contract was signed between George and Newton's American Marine Limited, and work began immediately on this new sailing vessel.

As the idea of their voyage became more and more real, a lot of thought went into the selection of additional crew members. George and Steve knew that two people could probably sail a boat of this size fairly easily, but not for a trip of such a duration. There would be many days of sailing across long, uninterrupted stretches of open sea, and they would need at least two more crew members to spell them in shifts.

George and Steve struggled to come up with names of people they could ask as potential crew, so they started asking around. But each time they approached someone, he had a reason for not joining the adventure—a job, a girlfriend, or an inclination to get home to the United States more quickly. Mostly, George and Steve were looking for guys who could come up with a share of the money to invest in the boat. Other qualifications were secondary. In fact, there weren't other qualifications. On the positive side for any crew candidates, there was a strong likelihood that building a boat in the Orient and then selling it in the United States would reap a handsome profit. This was precisely the market that Bob Newton was catering to.

George then thought of Walter Banks, a buddy from his days at flight school in Pensacola. He remembered they were both gadget guys who loved to tinker with machines. They had even developed plans for starting a business when they completed their respective tours of duty. With this thought, George set about to contact his friend and ask him if he would join the crew. Walter accepted and began preparations for traveling to Hong Kong.

CHAPTER 4

WALT AND PAUL

Walter Banks was another military man. He followed in the footsteps of his dad, graduating from Clemson University in 1954 with a major in engineering. He decided to enlist in the navy following his older brother who had been a shipboard naval officer during World War II. Hearing his brother tell of his many adventures in Europe, including D-Day, Walt had developed a romanticized notion about being in the navy.

His first duty station was Newport, Rhode Island, for officer training. There he quickly learned the meaning of the phrase "at the convenience of the government." The navy needed pilots and, having excellent vision, Walt was a perfect candidate. He was tall and in good health. The guys who wore glasses went to sea in ships and submarines. Walt took to the skies, learning to fly in Pensacola, Florida, and Corpus Christi, Texas.

Walt in navy flying school; Pensacola, Florida

Upon completion of flight training, Walt was ordered to Navy Attack Squadron 215 which was attached to Carrier Air Group 21. He was initially stationed at Moffett Field near Palo Alto, California. When the air group completed its training cycle, they boarded the aircraft carrier USS *Lexington* for an eight-month operational cruise to the western Pacific. They were part of about a hundred pilots and aircraft making up four squadrons based on the *Lexington.*

Walt's assigned aircraft was the Douglas AD6 Skyraider, the last propeller-driven plane flown from an aircraft carrier that could have delivered a nuclear weapon. These squadrons had a one-pilot, one-plane mission sometimes referred to as a "one-way ride" because their slow planes would not have been able to drop the bomb and still be quick enough to escape the atomic blast. Walt was hardly thrilled with that possibility.

Luckily, the world was a relatively peaceful place at that time. Had these pilots been called upon to do the job they were trained for, they would have flown from the carrier to the USSR or China to drop nuclear weapons on strategic enemy targets. As it was, the pilots spent most of their days flying practice missions all over the south Pacific. Practice missions were fine with Walt, as flying was a welcome break from the monotony of life aboard an aircraft carrier in peacetime.

After his active duty obligation was met, Walt returned to California and obtained an engineering position with Varian Associates of Palo Alto. His engineering group carried out technical upgrades of microwave components destined for the Dewline, a radar-based aircraft early warning system of the Cold War era. With his new job, Walt needed a place to live, so he answered a newspaper ad to rent a room in a house on Oregon Avenue in Palo Alto. The owner was Paul Cardoza.

Paul was a former military man as well, but his service predated the others' by almost a decade. He did his basic training in Ft. Hood, Texas, at the tail end of World War II and sailed to Japan on the *General Mann* shortly after V-J Day. After serving in Occupied Japan, he returned to his family's farm in Palo Alto and enrolled in San Jose State University on the GI bill. Over the next six years, he balanced schoolwork with his farm chores and a job at the post office. After getting his degree in business, Paul entered a management-training program with Standard Oil of California.

Following his father's passing, Paul's family sold their farm and bought two small houses. Paul and his wheelchair-bound mother moved into one of the houses and rented out the other. His oldest sister was over fifty and not in the best of health herself, but she helped their mother on weekends. His other three sisters lived hundreds of miles away and couldn't help out in any practical way. Paul's brothers lived nearby, but had large families and demanding jobs. In 1955, at the age of seventy, his mother passed away. Paul purchased the three-bedroom house he was living in from the estate. It was in this house that Walter Banks rented a room and became friends with Paul.

While Walt and Paul were in California, George and Steve were in Hong Kong working on the boat and gathering provisions. In frequent conversations, Walt would apprise Paul of the current state of preparations for the sailing voyage. At one point Walt suggested, "Why don't you join us?" Paul was interested in the whole idea, but at first he rejected it because of personal finances, career, and home ownership.

Finally, Walt told Paul that he would be leaving for Hong Kong. This impending departure led Paul to consider taking out a loan on his house to fund his portion of the adventure. Steve and George had been scraping together their one-third ownerships by selling nearly everything they had accumulated in the Philippines, including their automobiles. Luckily, they sold everything at a good price. Paul and Walt would have to contribute one-sixth interest each.

Freed from his family obligations, Paul decided to throw caution to the wind. Initially, he viewed this sailing adventure as something crazy that only a young kid would do, and he was an adult with grown-up responsibilities. Soon, though, the idea began to take up residence in his imagination. It wasn't long before the adventure became irresistible.

Chapter 5

A Fine Vessel

Amerikan Marine Limited was a new boatyard situated on Junk Bay in Hong Kong's New Territories on the mainland. As George and Steve headed out of their Kowloon apartment most mornings, a picturesque twenty-minute bus ride took them over the rolling landscape to Junk Bay. At the crest of the hill, before heading down to the boatyard, they could see the outer reaches of Hong Kong Harbor surrounded by hills in every direction.

Idyllic vista, American Marine Limited boatyard; Kowloon, Hong Kong

They traveled to the yard nearly every day to scrutinize the work being done on the boat that would take them home to America. They hired a marine surveyor to make sure she was built to Sparkman & Stephens' specifications. The help that George and Steve offered never involved actual construction of the wooden elements of the boat, rather, they were there to make decisions and chase down parts and equipment they would need for the voyage.

Most importantly they needed lead—nearly 6,500 pounds of it for the boat's keel. Lead was expensive in Hong Kong. Fortunately, George's position at Sangley Point made it easy for him to arrange trips back and forth to Hong Kong to check on the boat's progress. On a number of those trips from Manila, he and Steve transported carry-on bags containing lead that they were able to acquire for next to nothing from sources in the Philippines. The only real challenge was moving it between countries.

The weight of the lead was no problem for Steve because he had developed good upper body strength during his wrestling years at Yale. He just casually walked past all the entry points with a bag in each hand. The bags appeared to be of reasonable weight. However, when the Chinese porters attempted to assist him with his luggage, the bags slipped out of their hands and crashed to the ground. The porters couldn't believe how heavy they were! In all, George and Steve were able to transport about 400 pounds of lead to Hong Kong in this manner. Not the mother lode, but somewhat entrepreneurial.

American Marine Limited arranged for George and Steve to have a berth for their boat next to the one where construction on Max von Sydow's boat was taking place. It was a huge help to them because any mistakes made in building the actor's boat could be discovered and corrected before being repeated on their boat. In addition, Max von Sydow had all of his Merriman marine fittings available there at the boatyard. George or Steve would borrow them, one or two at a time, and head to the city to have them duplicated. Merriman fittings were considered the world's best boat hardware. They also carried a hefty price tag, well beyond what the new adventurers could afford. Having them copied in Hong Kong brought their price to a quarter of what they would have otherwise cost. The cast brass and bronze parts were functionally the same (at least they hoped they were); the average person couldn't tell them apart.

The guys' boat was designed by one of the world's finest ocean racing sailboat designers, Sparkman & Stephens of New York. The plans (design number 1380) cost $500. Sparkman & Stephens also designed the *Finisterre*, arguably the top-racing sailboat of the twentieth century. Launched in 1954, the *Finisterre* won the distinction of First in Class and First Overall in three consecutive Bermuda races (1956, 1958, 1960)—a feat that had never before been achieved. This rather small vessel, with an LOA (length overall) of 38 feet, was a beamy bronze centerboard yawl that combined seaworthiness with comfort and speed, especially in light winds. A great racing boat under all conditions, the *Finisterre* had the greatest theoretical hull speed of any similar boat at that time.

All sails on *Finisterre*—full and by

The boat being built for the Americans had many of the same characteristics as the *Finisterre*, except theirs was a keeled boat, differing from the *Finisterre's* centerboard design. Their boat drew six feet of water and had 6,500 lbs. of lead built into the keel.

To calculate the amount of time it would take to sail from Hong Kong to Miami, the crew needed to know how fast the boat could sail. The formula to calculate a theoretical speed through the water is 1.34 times the square root of the waterline length. The waterline length of this particular boat was to be 27.5 feet. Thus, the formula was 1.34 x 5.244=7.03 mph. In a light breeze, it could move along easily at 4½ miles per hour. In theory, doubling the wind force should mean that a boat would go twice as fast, but in truth this formula follows the law of diminishing returns. An increase in wind force does not mean the boat's speed increases to an equal degree. Their boat would never manage much above six miles per hour in good weather, and less in stormy seas.

The boat was a yawl design, 40.5 feet in length, 27.5 feet on the water, with a 10-foot, 6-inch beam and a 55-foot mast. A yawl has a second mast (mizzenmast) aft of the helm that is much shorter than the main mast and serves to balance the helm in varying sea conditions. A yawl has a minimum of three sails fore to aft: a Genoa jib, a main, and a mizzen.

Fitting out *Suzy Wong* for launching; Junk Bay, Hong Kong

In addition to the basic design rights for their boat, George and Steve received detailed working drawings of the hull, standing rigging, and a sail plan. For the most part, these plans were done well. However, the drawings and specs did not include design engineering and communication systems. The crew designed and built these systems themselves with ample help from American Marine Limited and the US Navy.

The water system was basic. The crew would have to hand-pump water from the two fifty-gallon, tin-lined copper tanks located under the bunks in the main cabin. The fuel system consisted of a hundred-gallon fuel tank of similar copper material under the cockpit.

The boat's electrical system was cobbled together using castoff components and batteries salvaged from a US Navy Martin Mariner seaplane that had crashed in the Philippines. A communications officer for the Far East gave the crew a radio transmitter. It was reported to have belonged to a World War II Japanese spy who was presumably captured and executed. The old-fashioned transmitter was crystal controlled and operated only with Morse code, so communication would be difficult.

Steve had been the first to take up residence in Hong Kong, renting a small room in a boardinghouse. George came shortly after his trip home to see his mother. When Walt arrived, he settled in with George and Steve in a newly rented apartment. Meanwhile, Paul was getting his affairs in order in California.

Walter arrived in time to help George order the engine and other mechanical equipment. They settled on a small Stuart Turner diesel marine engine from England. The rigging cables were ordered from New York. Knowing the dynamics of a sailboat, they concluded that they couldn't cut corners when it came to the rigging. They were willing to pay a higher price to ensure their safety at sea.

When the rigging arrived, George and Walter had to fasten end connectors to the rigging cables, often referred to as stays. These fittings had to be pressure squeezed, or swedged, onto the cable ends. (Swedging is a procedure that bonds a cable end fitting to a cable using a die press and applying extreme pressure.) Only one end of each stay had been swedged by the manufacturer in New York because cables have to be cut to an exact length. So George and Walter made arrangements to have the other end-fittings swedged at the Kai Tak Airport in Honk Kong, where large aircraft have their control cable connectors secured in a similar manner. The airport had the equipment and the know-how to do the job.

The Kai Tak Airport accepted the assignment, and the work was completed without delay. Walter asked the airport engineer if they had tested the strength of the swedged connections. Surprisingly, the answer was, "No." Walter then asked to have one of the cables tested to its design strength. It failed the test. The end connector easily pulled off the stay. It turned out that the airport's swedging machine was worn and hadn't done a proper job. After adjusting their machine, they were able to complete the work. Had Walter not insisted on testing the stay connections, the first stiff breeze would have certainly cost them their mast, and possibly their lives.

Chapter 6

The Chinese Boatyard

For the three Americans, observing the Chinese at work became a major source of fascination and wonder. In building these wooden boats, all kinds of rare woods were used. The initial keel, or "dead wood," used as a boat's foundation was made from pieces of wood 10 inches x 10 inches x 20 feet in length. Bow and sternposts were made from husky pieces of hardwood. The frame ribs were made from long black 2 x 2-inch strips of Philippine ipe wood, which was many times harder than oak, earning it the name "ironwood." This wood was so dense that it sank in water. In order to bend it to form the frames, it had to be placed in a steam box for two days. The boat's planking was made of 1¼-inch Burma teak.

To Western eyes, the complete absence of electric-powered tools for cutting or forming any of the lumber was a source of amazement. Saw cuts were simply made by a handsaw. Drill holes were made by a bow and spindle hand-drill. The patience required to form the wooden parts of the boat was phenomenal. To the Chinese, it was standard procedure.

The interior of the boat boasted a hand-rubbed lacquer finish. Chinese craftsmen had carved two opposing dragons into an overhead piece of teak that one would see when coming down the hatchway. Dragons in China are considered to be divine, mythical creatures that bring abundance, prosperity, and good luck. The sailors enjoyed these details and felt a certain security in having the dragons aboard.

While Chinese workers performed most of the labor, the three Americans were very much involved with the technical aspects of the boat. In fact, George designed the dorade vents—the baffled ventilators that allow fresh air into the cabin below, even in bad weather, without letting water in. Dorade vents are usually plain, round, and uninteresting. George's design was visually stunning: elliptical in shape, shining chrome on the outside, and painted a bright red on the inside. In short, his vents were works of art.

Workday at the boatyard, Paul on deck; Junk Bay, Hong Kong

A lot happened under the watchful eyes of the visiting foreign crew members. They could understand and enjoy many aspects of the daily routine of the boatyard, but other subtleties were beyond their ability to grasp given their limited familiarity with Chinese culture. Only one Chinese worker, the yard foreman, spoke English. This didn't really impede work on the boat, as both groups, the American and the Chinese, worked in their own sphere of expertise.

One of the characteristics of the Chinese workmen at the yard was their love of gambling and chance. To relax during their noon-hour break, they played a game of rolling coins down an inclined board onto the cement floor. The point of the game was to see who could roll his coin the farthest before it fell over and stopped. They hooted and hollered each time a coin rolled past another's. At the end, there was an exchange of money.

A modest initial launching of the boat occurred one night at the end of a busy day with only the Chinese workers and the young sailors present. Its purpose was to move the boat out from under the shed where it had been built and onto an outside slip where the mast and rigging could be installed. This launch was deemed successful. It was, after all, the first test of the boat's seaworthiness.

CHAPTER 7

HONG KONG LIFE

The density of humanity added richly to Hong Kong's unique urban character. On any given street, the start or end of a workday would see thousands of people bursting forth from buildings, like ants erupting from an anthill. Elegant British colonial structures stood beside the austere concrete boxes that served as homes for the Chinese families. The oppressive structural heaviness was only occasionally alleviated by hundreds of delicate Buddhist temples tucked away in tiny spaces throughout the city. The walkways along the harbor offered the only hint of open space. Even the waterways were congested, with hundreds of the iconic bat-winged Chinese boats, called junks, struggling to navigate around each other.

Iconic Chinese junk; Hong Kong

Paul arrived in Hong Kong in December 1959, and the crew of four former American servicemen came together for the first time. A betting person would have given these four men absolutely no chance of succeeding in realizing their dream. Many blue-water sailing cruises don't make it past their first port of call due to personality differences. This assembled crew hardly knew each other, certainly adding to the challenge ahead of them. George had never met Paul, Walter had never met Steve, and Paul had never met either Steve or George.

Their grand adventure together began by sharing a small apartment in Kowloon. The apartment was on the second floor of a four-story building on Cameron Road. A young prostitute named Lulu lived and worked in the vicinity of the apartment. Steve and Paul befriended her and would hail her in passing with, "How's business?" She always responded cheerfully by telling them which US Navy ships were in port at the time.

Directly across the street from the apartment was the Palm Court Hotel where the four ate breakfast every morning. It was ostensibly a British hotel, but all the employees were Chinese, so communication was difficult at best. The crew always ordered oatmeal because it was the cheapest thing on the menu. Unfortunately, the Chinese weren't used to hearty American appetites, so each serving consisted of a modest portion of oatmeal lumped at the bottom of a very large bowl. Paul tried once to explain to the restaurant personnel that they all wanted a "full bowl." The Chinese must have thought "full bowl" was some kind of strange Yankee term for oatmeal because they nodded their heads as if in agreement that, yes, the Americans were indeed eating "full bowls." The restaurant never did change the portion size, and the crew remained hungry after every breakfast.

From the outset, the stage was set for the crew members' different personalities to show themselves. George was busy taking in the entire enterprise. He was responsible for selecting the boatyard and the boat design. He was always dreaming up interesting flourishes such as the design of the dorade vents or the addition of carved dragons in the overhead as one descends into the main cabin from the cockpit.

Walter focused on the technical aspects of the project such as the selection of the engine, the rigging strength, and the route they would eventually take heading west around the world. He was a man of few words and resolute action.

Steve was adventuresome and willing to apply his talents wherever needed. He took on the task of finding parts and having things made in Hong Kong. He was also the person to manage the money and keep track of expenses, although they didn't have much of a spending plan other than to keep costs to a minimum.

Paul, the last to sign up for the expedition, was the jokester of the four. He had developed card tricks while in the army and he presented them masterfully, keeping secret how he was able to fool his audience. On top of that, he had an endless supply of jokes stored away in his head. Meeting and greeting people of all backgrounds and descriptions were Paul's special talents. If Steve was the trip's financial record keeper, Paul was its social secretary.

The soon-to-be ocean travelers began provisioning for their westward voyage. They stored food supplies (mostly canned goods) on the floor of their apartment. Hong Kong had water rationing in those days, making water available for only a few designated hours each day. On one memorable occasion, someone forgot the hour and turned on the faucet to shower. No water came out, but the guilty party (it was never determined exactly who) forgot to turn off the faucet. When the water was made available again, the apartment flooded. The front door fit so snugly that the water stayed in the apartment until Paul returned home and opened the door. The water poured out, drenching him. The parquet squares on the floor floated around his feet, along with all the identifying labels from the food cans.

The men were panic-stricken that they had ruined the floor. Their landlord, Peter Chung, was a friendly man with an interest in their forthcoming voyage. He had helped with many contacts throughout the city. Peter was an affable sort under most circumstances, always smiling and speaking softly to convey that he was their friend. However, he was still their landlord and, like most landlords, he didn't want to spend his hard-earned money on repairs of any kind. He was not happy that the Americans flooded his apartment, and he grudgingly hired someone to glue the parquet tiles back onto the floor. The floor problem could be fixed, but what was in each of the cans of food would remain a mystery until they were opened.

In addition to food, the crew needed to collect proper clothing and safety equipment for the voyage. In early conversations they discussed a need for weapons. Before leaving California to join the others, Paul decided that he wanted to bring his own firearm. He had a friend named Ken Russell who was affectionately known as "Runt," despite being six feet, eight inches tall. Paul went to him for advice since Runt and his father were both gun collectors. They talked about the kind of weapon Paul should take on board and what kind he could bring into Hong Kong. A rifle or shotgun was out of the question. Runt said, "I have a WWI .45 revolver. It's old, but extremely effective and will blow the shit out of anything it hits." Then he said, "There'll be a hole about the size of a nickel in the front of whatever you shoot, and a hole a foot in diameter on the other side."

Runt loaded his own ammunition, filling the empty shells with gunpowder and a bullet head. Along with the gun, he gave Paul about three-dozen of his bullets. Paul packed the gun and supplies in his suitcase and hoped he would never have to use this relic of a firearm.

Walt took a Winchester 30/30 and a handgun into Hong Kong with his luggage. Steve and George came up with an old Italian rifle, a shotgun, and a third handgun. They managed to slip the handguns past airport security in their luggage since screening of luggage was sparse in those days. The rifle and shotgun had been brought in as personal items from Sangley Point in the Philippines. All of these firearms were completely illegal in Hong Kong. Without question, the crew would be suitably armed, albeit with a mismatched hodgepodge of weaponry.

The four men worked on their boat each day. To get to the American Marine boatyard, they first took a city bus and then walked down a long, steep path through the small town of Hang Hao. Then a short walk down the main street of town took them into a big crowd of people, especially children, as well as dogs, pigs, and chickens. The scent of sandalwood arose from the open storefronts, and the smell of tofu filled the air with that distinct Chinese aroma. Finally, they'd come to a pier extending about fifty feet into the bay.

At the end of the pier, four or five women with sampans would vie for the chance to row the Americans across Junk Bay to the boatyard. It was a small bay that was easy to walk around, but it was quicker and more fun to take a hand-propelled water taxi to the boatyard. The female rowers charged five cents for each boat trip and elbowed each other out of the way to get the business, which might be their only fare all day.

The four Americans devised some gambling incentives to see whose boat would get their business for the day. The women would draw straws, pick numbers, or play some other game of chance. The women were intently involved in the process and completely understood what was going on, despite the language barrier. They seemed to love the daily exchange they had with the four young Americans.

The guys were fascinated by the Chinese boat people living on their junks in the colorfully named Gin Drinkers Bay. Even traveling to the boat each day became an indelible part of the experience. While the Americans couldn't converse with the locals in Chinese, they developed their own means of communication. Like a schoolboy pulling a prank, George would greet the bus driver each morning by pointing to his head and repeating the single Chinese phrase he had learned from them—"muk tau," which means "wooden head" in Cantonese. Then they both would smile in acknowledgement of a shared joke.

CHAPTER 8

THE WORLD OF SUZIE WONG

In 1957, Hong Kong was an exotic place that most Americans never expected to visit, yet they still felt they had a pretty good idea of what it must be like. Many of those preconceptions came from the novel *The World of Suzie Wong* by British author Richard Mason.

The novel was a romance story about a young Englishman, Robert Lomax, who decides to pursue a career as an artist. Visiting Hong Kong for inspiration, Lomax checks into a hotel, not realizing it is a brothel. This detail only makes the hotel more charming in Lomax's opinion, and a better source of subject matter for his paintings. Soon, Lomax meets Suzie Wong. Suzie Wong turns out to be a prostitute, but the two nevertheless develop an attraction that is mutual and genuine.

Early book reviews were kind, though hardly enthusiastic, praising Mason particularly for his progressive treatment (for its time) of the Asian culture and the profession of prostitution. Fueling "yellow fever"—the attraction some Western men felt for exotic Asian women—the book became an international bestseller and a guilty pleasure for men and women alike.

Shortly after the novel was published, playwright Paul Osborn wrote a stage version of *The World of Suzie Wong*. The play opened on Broadway at New York's Broadhurst Theatre on October 14, 1958, starring a young William Shatner as Robert Lomax and France Nuyen as Suzie Wong.

While expectations were high, the audience began leaving mid-show. The director had turned the romantic script into a turgid melodrama. Behind-the-scenes, France Nuyen wanted the director off the set. She threatened to stop speaking if he ever came back to the theater.

It wasn't long before Nuyen saw the director lurking in the wings and, following through on her threat, she simply refused to say her lines. A desperate

Shatner sped up his lines to a ridiculous tempo, changing the intonation and emotion in the process so he could quickly finish and get off stage. Then a curious thing happened…the audience began to laugh.

At the next evening's performance, Shatner and Nuyen decided to play the entire show tongue-in-cheek, strongly suggesting to audiences that this was not a show to be taken seriously. Audiences began to think of the show as a funny and sweet romantic comedy. Word got around that the play was a hit and, instead of closing early, it ran for a full fourteen months.

Not surprisingly, Paramount Pictures was next in line. They bought the film rights to produce a Hollywood version of *The World of Suzie Wong*. With Academy Award winner William Holden in the leading role, the movie would be all the rage.

While the sailors were hard at work on their boat and making final preparations for their voyage, Paramount Pictures came to Hong Kong to do the location shooting for its new movie. Having Hollywood in Hong Kong was a big event for the Chinese. The movie title itself became omnipresent. Namesakes were beginning to pop up everywhere as the Chinese named foods, goods, and services after the movie.

The crew frequented a restaurant, a dive called Rikki's, that didn't know how to make a decent tossed salad. Frustrated, Paul went into the kitchen one day to show them how it was done. He made an ordinary salad—just lettuce, tomato, cucumber, and a dressing of oil and vinegar—but the restaurant liked it so much that they put it on their menu as the "Suzie Wong Salad." The guys now had their first connection to the story of Suzie Wong.

CHAPTER 9

A CHANCE MEETING

Steve had his own encounter with the Suzie Wong movie in the Peninsula Hotel. Established in 1928, The Peninsula Hotel had become synonymous with unsurpassed luxury and service. The hotel's restaurant, bar, and lobby were elegantly draped in velvety fabrics and well-appointed with overstuffed, tufted sofas and easy chairs. The sound of live music from a grand piano or small string ensemble drifted through the public rooms. Home away from home for the rich and famous, the Peninsula was William Holden's favorite place to indulge in cocktails.

One afternoon Steve Jackson visited The Peninsula and spotted Holden across the bar. The actor was approachable and seemed an agreeable sort of fellow, and soon Steve was chatting with a world-famous movie star. Holden was a heavy smoker, prodigious drinker, and a big talker. He believed himself to be a raconteur, telling witty stories about Hollywood. One didn't have a conversation with William Holden. He talked; you listened. Mostly, he just talked about himself. When Steve could get a word in edgewise, he mentioned his upcoming voyage. Holden seemed interested, if only casually. Steve came away from the meeting not remembering much of the movie star's droning monologue, only that they had met and chatted over a drink or two. What he did take away, however, had more lasting value—it was a name for their boat!

Given Steve's encounter with Holden and the general buzz about the film shoot, it was only natural that the crew thought of *The World of Suzie Wong* when it came time to name their boat. Although they tossed around a lot of possibilities, the crew quickly decided that naming the boat after the movie's title character was as good a plan as any. After all, ship owners frequently named their boats after women, and the movie would serve as an affectionate reminder of their embarkation point in Hong Kong.

George was the man who drew up the initial plans for the voyage and did the crew's graphic work. When laying out the new name of the boat, George took it upon himself to change the spelling of the title character's first name—from Suzie to Suzy—for aesthetic reasons. He felt the shortened version would be more symmetrical and look better painted onto the ship's transom. Steve strongly argued that they should christen the boat with the name spelled exactly as used in the movie. Paul and Walt agreed with George, so the majority ruled. The boat affectionately became known as the *Suzy Wong*.

CHAPTER 10

THE STAR FERRY

In each of its incarnations as a book, play, and movie, *The World of Suzie Wong* introduced its two leading characters in an extended opening scene aboard the *Star Ferry* in Hong Kong. Established in 1888, the *Star Ferry* was the only public means of transportation between Hong Kong Island and the Kowloon Peninsula. A ride aboard the *Star Ferry* was arguably the cheapest multicultural and multisensory cruise experience in the world. It provided great views of the city skyline, the hills of Kowloon, and a glimpse into the lifestyle of Hong Kong residents—all for just fifty cents.

On January 30, the crew boarded the *Star Ferry* going to Junk Bay where Max von Sydow was launching his new boat, the sister ship of the *Suzy Wong*. *Suzy* was still far from completion and already several weeks behind schedule. Nevertheless, the crew was in high spirits. They were going to get a glimpse of what their boat would look like on the water. They also knew that the launching of von Sydow's boat meant that the builder, Bob Newton, would now have more time to spend on *Suzy Wong*.

Standing upon the ferry's deck, the crew spotted a beautiful, tall, blond woman. Mary DeForest stood out like a solitary daffodil on a gloomy spring day. The four guys jockeyed for an opportunity to chat with her, but Mary seemed enchanted with Paul. After some small talk, Paul invited her to join them at the launching party. She responded, "I was going to visit a friend, but she's not feeling well." And then, surprisingly, "Yes, I'd like to go."

Like Paul, Mary was from California. She worked for the Foreign Service and was completing a two-year post at the US Embassy in Cambodia. Mary was in Hong Kong for ten days of rest and relaxation before being reassigned to the US Embassy in Spain.

Mary wrote her mother,

> I met a group of young fellows who are having a boat built here in
> Hong Kong and then they are going to set sail around the world. It
> sounds like a wild scheme, but actually they appear to be quite well
> organized about their trip and well prepared.

Paul and Mary spent much of the next week together. Paul introduced her to an Indian tailor and to the Chinese carver who had done some of the detailed woodwork on the *Suzy Wong*. They each ordered rosewood furniture and had matching garden motifs carved into it. Then Mary agreed to ship his furniture back to California with her things. In the evenings they shared meals together and listened to music and danced.

On the weekend they took an overnight boat to Macau together with Steve and his parents, who had come to Hong Kong to see their son before the voyage. When they returned from exploring the Portuguese colony in Macau, Steve's folks invited all the boys and Mary to their hotel-apartment for dinner. Paul did the cooking. On the menu was stuffed pork chops, string beans with bacon, baked potatoes with sour cream, and, of course, his Suzie Wong salad— all well prepared and presented. "He's really excellent in the kitchen and loves it," Mary later wrote home.

On their last evening together, Paul took Mary to a small restaurant on Hong Kong's Victoria Peak overlooking the Hong Kong Harbor and Kowloon. The night was clear and the lights were dazzling. After dinner, they walked down from the Peak on a winding, wooded pathway and finished up at a nightclub near the water. The *Star Ferry* had long since shut down for the night, but it would figure significantly in the history of their relationship. Paul had fallen head-over-heels for Mary; now she was all he could think about. They promised to write often and planned to see each other again when Paul and the crew reached Spain.

CHAPTER 11

THE PUBLICIST

As they continued to work on their boat, George, Steve, Walt, and Paul would make another important contact in that of a public relations man from Manhattan. Irving Hoffman was a superb publicity agent. For the first twenty years of his career, he was a theater critic and columnist for *The Hollywood Reporter*. His showbiz background and aggressive reporting style made for a natural transition into his next positions as freelance publicist and press agent. Although he worked behind the scenes, Hoffman became nearly as famous in his own right as the actors he covered.

Hoffman's physical countenance belied his shark-like professional reputation. He wore glasses with lenses as thick as the bottom of soda bottles to correct his extreme near-sighted vision. When Hoffman wrote a scathing review of the play *Ethan Frome* in 1931, producer Max Gordon complained that Hoffman was physically unqualified for his job because he "can't see." Hoffman squinted agreeably and said, "Yes, but there's nothing wrong with my nose!" With all his experience and personality, it was no wonder that Paramount Pictures hired Hoffman to write profile features on their upcoming movie, *The World of Suzie Wong*.

At roughly the same time that Steve accidentally met William Holden, Paul bumped into Irving Hoffman. The two men had a brief conversation during which Hoffman stated simply that he was working on the film *The World of Suzie Wong*. In his amiable and polite manner, Paul informed Hoffman that he and three other American servicemen had named their boat the *Suzy Wong* and were about to embark on a worldwide voyage. Paul didn't have to say much more for Hoffman's mind to shift into overdrive. Hoffman felt there was something wonderfully odd in the story of four guys sailing halfway around the world in a boat named after a movie. So he concocted an arrangement (most likely without any consent from Paramount Pictures) to create additional publicity for *The World of Suzie Wong* using the *Suzy Wong*.

The arrangement was simple: All the guys had to do was get the words "*Suzy Wong*" or "*Suzie Wong*" in print in any newspaper, anywhere around the world, and they would be paid fifty dollars per article. Hoffman would do a little advance work as well, that of informing the press ahead of time in destinations where the sailors intended to make port along their journey. Hoffman thought the crew might find it fun to be connected to a motion picture. Worried about finances, the crew was more interested in the chance to make a few extra bucks for their cash-strapped trip. It never occurred to them that the publicity Hoffman generated for the *Suzy Wong* would have much more value than the money.

CHAPTER 12

GETTING ACQUAINTED

This entire adventure would have seemed like a natural if the four Americans had been long-time buddies who knew each other's characters and quirks. But before coming together in Hong Kong, these guys were mostly strangers to each other. They were comprised of a New Yorker, a Californian, and two Southerners; one from Virginia and one from North Carolina. Two were army men; two were navy men. The four crew members had little in common beyond their shared military training. Given the long voyage ahead of them, it was highly fortunate that they just meshed well from the beginning.

George Todd had a gregarious nature, borne out of his mother's Southern gentility and his father's small-town ease of dealing with people. George was always the first to greet strangers and include them in his circle. People were just drawn to him. George was born on December 20, 1931, in Norfolk, Virginia. His mother, Consuela, was on a women's basketball team back in the days when female players still wore bloomers. She became seriously ill with polio shortly after George was born and spent seven years in the hospital. A nanny did most of his childrearing, but he remembers his mother as having impeccable manners.

George's father was from Norfolk and worked as a lawyer. When his wife became ill, he needed a less-stressful career, one that would allow him to stay closer to home; so he went to work for an insurance company as a trouble-shooter. Following his father's sudden death, George had to step up and become the man of the family at the age of fifteen. Despite his adult responsibility of taking care of his mother, George continued to nurture his sensitive, artistic side. He realized as a kid that he was good at drawing and he loved to paint; he even won a first-place prize for one of his oil paintings.

Just as his art skills would come in handy when designing the boat's dorade vents, George's mechanical aptitude would also prove valuable on the voyage. He was building a racecar when he first met Walter Banks. Both were in the US Navy in Pensacola. One day while under his car tinkering with the motor, George saw these huge feet coming toward his face. The feet stopped a couple of inches from his head, and a drawling Chattanooga voice said, "Maybe there's something I could help you with there." George scooted out and looked up at six-and-a-half-foot-tall Walter Banks smiling down at him.

Walter was the technical expert of the bunch, a do-everything kind of guy who could learn something from scratch or by trial and error. Walter Banks Jr. was born February 1, 1932, in Charlotte, North Carolina. His parents, both originally natives of South Carolina, had migrated farther north by the time Walt came along.

With a degree in mechanical engineering, Walt Sr. worked at the Ford Motor Company in Charlotte until the company ceased operations there. He then worked for the Tennessee Valley Authority for the rest of his career. The TVA constructed dams and associated infrastructure along the Tennessee River from its headwaters in the Shenandoah Valley to its confluence with the Ohio River in Kentucky. The family moved often in Walt junior's early years, forcing him to change schools and prove himself to his new classmates over and over. Accordingly, he fought his way across many a schoolyard.

Walt's mother, Constance, had an advanced degree in mathematics from the University of South Carolina, but she decided that raising her family was more important than a possible career in her chosen field. When World War II started, Constance took a job with the Red Cross to help returning soldiers deal with problems at home. She parlayed this into a career as a social worker helping other people in need, particularly providing shelter for unwed mothers.

Walt Jr. attended his father's alma mater, Clemson University, even graduating with the same degree in mechanical engineering. He was a good student, but the information he preferred was the kind he didn't find in books. Walt loved to tinker. Every machine he came across was a puzzle to be taken apart, understood, and put back together. After his military service, Walt returned to Palo Alto, where he was first stationed, to take a job as an engineer with a manufacturing company. It was in Palo Alto that Walt became acquainted with Paul.

Paul Cardoza may have been the last man to sign on to the *Suzy Wong*, but his lifelong disciplined work ethic would be a strong addition to the crew. Paul was born on January 27, 1927, in Palo Alto, California, the seventh child of immigrant parents from the Azores. Although they never had much money to spare, his parents were hard-working and eventually managed to purchase a few acres of farmland. The entire family was expected to work at something.

From a young age, Paul worked at various jobs. He sold fresh vegetables from his parents' garden off the back of a wagon. He also peddled magazines and newspapers on University Avenue in Palo Alto. Up at 5:30 every morning, he rode his bike along unlit roads to the train station to sell his copies of the *San Francisco Chronicle* and the *Examiner*. Paul learned that customers preferred to buy from energetic, gregarious, and polite newsboys, so he always worked on enhancing those qualities.

Paul's parents were not formally educated and because they were always focused on surviving, they never gave a high priority to Paul's academic abilities. But Paul was smart, and his parents instilled in their son a strong work ethic and the desire to contribute to the support and wellbeing of the family.

Paul's mother was in her early forties when Paul was born, so he had no memory of her as a robust, young farmwoman. As Paul grew older and stronger, his mother's health gradually declined; she suffered from crippling arthritis. Over the years, her illness progressed, taking her from a cane to a wheelchair, and then finally she became bedridden. Yet she never lost her mental acuity or vital spirit, and Paul felt that he found his own inner strength from her example.

While Paul was the oldest member of the crew, Steve Jackson was the youngest, born on October 20, 1934, in South Salem, New York. He grew up in a rambunctious household of three boys, with an older brother, Robert Jr., and a younger brother, Spencer. One night when Steve was seven, his mother, Laura, had all three boys in the bathtub when his father rushed into the bathroom and announced excitedly, "The Japs have bombed Pearl Harbor!" Laura responded, "Don't bother me now, Bob. Can't you see I'm busy?"

Raising three boys all close in age was a lot for Laura to handle, and she always had to break up fights between Steve and Robert. There was never much danger of blood being spilt, but those family fisticuffs helped form Steve's independence. One summer, years later, Steve, Spencer, and friend, John Choate, heard of available jobs in Oregon's lumber industry, so they hopped in Steve's father's old 1946 Plymouth and started driving across the country. They were in Montana when they got word of an Oregon lumber strike, so they just stopped where they were and found jobs working as ranch hands instead.

Tired of being treated poorly, Steve soon left the ranch and took a different job with a seismic surveying team before heading back to college in the fall. At Yale, Steve made the wrestling team, with an undefeated record his senior year. Growing up with two brothers had taught him to be competitive; wrestling built his physical strength and reinforced his confidence in handling difficult situations.

One of the many other pursuits that greatly interested Steve over the years was photography. In high school, he managed to talk the principal into letting him take all of his classmates' yearbook pictures instead of hiring a professional photographer. From the time he was assigned military duties in the Philippines, he took hundreds of pictures. His independence, adventurous spirit, confidence, strength, and love of photography would be great assets on the voyage ahead.

CHAPTER 13

SUZY GETS A MASCOT

The crew had contracted for the boat to be shipshape and ready to sail by the first of January 1960. This launch date would have timed them well for the weather ahead. They weren't experienced sailors, but they did have a vague sense of the dangers involved with the monsoons in Southeast Asia and the summer hurricane season in the Atlantic. Mostly, the crew just wanted to get going sooner rather than later because they were excited about the voyage ahead.

The projected price tag of the boat was $18,000. However, having a boat built in Hong Kong, or anywhere for that matter, had cost overrides just like any complicated project. By the time the boat was ready for departure from Hong Kong, the crew would owe the owner of the boatyard, Bob Newton, an additional $8,000. Newton agreed to this debt with a handshake, allowing the Americans to sail off and trusting that they would repay him at the end of their trip when they sold the boat.

The first of January came and went and by late February they were still waiting to depart. With their easygoing spirits, the crew didn't think this delay was a serious problem. Had they known how hard the monsoon winds would blow, they would have been far more concerned.

George and Walt had been trained as military aviators: they were used to making mental lists of "things that can kill you" when preparing aircraft for action. They carefully applied the same discipline to the preparation of the *Suzy Wong* and came up with a logical way to deal with difficult situations. They surmised that sailboats go about one-one hundredth the speed of airplanes, so if a problem arose they would simply take the time to look up answers in a handbook manual. This seemed a reasonable tactic when dealing with such an apparently leisurely mode of transportation.

A dog was not on the crew's list of provisions, but the boatyard owner's son, Whit, just happened to have a litter of puppies and he decided a dog would be a nice going-away present for the sailors. Whit brought the four-month-old Imperial Chinese Chow puppy with white fur and a black tongue down to the shipyard and the guys fell in love the moment they first saw him. These four tough ex-military men instantly turned into softies when presented with this adorable puppy, its tail wagging furiously and tongue working at a hundred licks a minute. The dog ran up to the group, licked them, jumped all around, and then peed on a shoe or two. He was a round blur of white fur, and he had stolen the sailors' hearts within seconds. So now, a month prior to setting sail, the *Suzy Wong* had acquired its mascot.

Mascot Gou eagerly stands watch; Junk Bay, Hong Kong

A number of sailing experts warned the *Suzy Wong* crew that taking a dog on the journey might not be a smart idea. For instance, no one had considered the practical matter of how the dog would relieve himself on board. Only four months old and still a puppy, he had not been potty trained and had never been on a boat before. The crew knew it was not practical to take him, but they had fallen in love with him and, in their minds, the dog was coming along. Like many of the crew's decisions, this one was made instantly and emotionally, not from a practical point of view.

Early suggestions for the puppy's name included something ferocious like "Sar Tao," which meant "killer" in Cantonese. Ultimately, his name became Gou, a Cantonese word meaning simply "dog," which the crew learned when the puppy got lost and the Chinese neighbors yelled "gou, gou, gou!" to help find him.

The night before setting sail on their journey, George and Walt were celebrating by having a few cocktails at the Palm Court Hotel. The subject turned to Gou and how the poor dog would relieve himself aboard the boat. George began a long dissertation about his views while Walt listened quietly for a while. Then he suddenly interrupted George and said, "I'm done talking about this!" He stood up, grabbed a potted palm tree from beside the table, and walked out. A short Chinese waiter ran behind him tugging on his coat, trying to get him to put down the plant. But Walt was tall and determined. He took the palm straight to the boat and placed it on the transom. Walt, being a man of action and few words, had implemented his idea for Gou's relief.

CHAPTER 14

THE GALA EVENT

The crew's original plan called for extensive sailing in and around Hong Kong and going out to sea for several nights to get used to the boat. As it turned out, they sailed for only a couple of days in the harbor area and never got around to undertaking any nighttime practice runs before departure. The reality was that there was extremely limited sailing experience among the group. Walt had spent nights at sea on an aircraft carrier, and Steve had sailed a small boat as a youth in addition to spending a week on the *Ping Po* a year earlier. Beyond that, the crew was made up of four complete novices!

Steve became a member of the Royal Hong Kong Yacht Club at the end of 1959, thinking this connection would be helpful throughout the voyage. Steve wrote to his parents on December 8, 1959: "Last night Bob Newton introduced me to the committee for membership into the Royal Hong Kong Yacht Club. This should give us the social ticket to various yacht clubs around the world. It will also enable us to use their facilities to keep us free of robbers."

The filming of the movie *The World of Suzie Wong* created such a stir in Hong Kong that the Chamber of Commerce decided to piggyback on the excitement in order to encourage boat building in the city. Having the *Suzy Wong* there and ready for launching was the perfect opportunity. The Chamber planned to charter the *Star Ferry* and host a grand party. The ferry would transport business dignitaries and other invited guests from Hong Kong to Junk Bay where the *Suzy Wong* would be put to sea.

The launching of the *Suzy Wong* on February 21, 1960, was a gala event with many respectable onlookers. She was festooned from the bow up to the top of the mast and then down to the stern with a string of colorful signal flags, one for every number between 1 and 10 and one for each letter in the alphabet.

Steve's parents, Robert and Laura Jackson, came to Hong Kong to meet Steve's crewmates and witness the launching. In grand style, Mrs. Jackson christened the *Suzy Wong* with a bottle of champagne, saying, "Wishing all who sail on her, fair winds and good fortune!" At that moment, the braking chocks were removed and the lovely lady slid into the water. Loud applause came from the many well-wishers gathered for the occasion—family and friends, Bob Newton's business acquaintances, yard workers, actor Max von Sydow, and publicist Irving Hoffman.

The four crew members and Gou were photographed like Hollywood stars with their wide smiles, crisp white shirts, coats, and ties. The Chinese boatyard workers, despite their meager wages, set off firecrackers to frighten away bad spirits and devils, which they considered a necessary part of the launching. The explosions filled the air around the boat with smoke and loud crackling sounds.

All hands, full dress for launching; Steve, Paul, Gou, Walt, and George

Publicist Irving Hoffman signed his bon voyage to the second page of the *Suzy Wong* guestbook. It was a brilliant red and black cartoon sketch of a voluptuous China doll in her cheongsam split skirt, looking very much like Suzie Wong sitting atop a boat's life preserver.

The big moment of their departure came on Sunday afternoon, March 6, 1960, ten months since the inception of the idea. Bob Newton and many of his workers were there to witness the start of the voyage. Over the course of the boat's construction, they had become friends with the four Americans and wanted to let the sailors know they would be praying for their safe passage. It was a beautiful afternoon with not a cloud in the sky. Reporters thronged the pier hoping to get last-minute access to the crew members, and another full display of firecrackers was set off. Junks, sampans, boats from the Royal Hong Kong Yacht Club, and Max von Sydow waving from *Suzy's* sister ship—all gathered to wish the adventurers bon voyage.

Although the crew members were happy and excited to finally get their journey under way, they might have felt just a hint of apprehension. From the very beginning, there had been an undercurrent of tension in every aspect of their preparations. If they were being honest, they would have had to admit that this adventure was truly a crazy idea. With the palm tree still on the stern of the boat, the *Suzy Wong* eagerly and naively sailed out of Hong Kong Harbor. They were finally on their way.

CHAPTER 15

SAILING AWAY

Within an hour of leaving the Royal Yacht Club pier, the *Suzy Wong* had sailed away from civilization toward darkness and open water. The ship's log recorded that the vessel "departed Hong Kong's inner harbor" at 1630h (4:30 p.m.). At 2200h the boat turned due south from Hong Kong heading for Manila, 180 degrees on the compass. It was their first night on board at sea.

Several experienced sailors advised the *Suzy Wong* crew that they should have a specific captain, one man in charge, but the crew chose to ignore this advice. Instead, they decided that whichever man was at the helm would be the captain for that time. If they had chosen only one captain, it probably would have been Walter Banks, who had been a naval officer with navigational experience and mechanical know-how. But everyone aboard felt that a military demeanor might put a crimp in the looseness the crew wanted. There was concern that a pleasurable vacation might turn into an unwanted tour of duty. Each man needed to be able to express himself freely without intimidation. These considerations made it imperative that each should have a leadership role in some way. Ultimately, the crew decided to have no single captain, thereby fostering a sense of equality (and hopefully harmony) on board the boat.

When blue-water sailing in the ocean, a crew almost never gets to hold up, or anchor, for the night. It's an around-the-clock endeavor. For the crew of four, this meant each of them was on the helm for six hours a day. They divided the helm duty by working in teams of two for six hours at a time. The team could break up their six hours any way they wanted.

This schedule meant that your turn at the helm could come at almost any time of day or night. You could be jolted from a sound sleep and have to emerge on deck on a dark, cold night to steer the designated course for the next three hours. It was scary, particularly at first, plowing ahead into the darkness and hoping you wouldn't run into anything like a partially submerged log or, even worse, a reef. On that first night at sea, they didn't trust anyone at the helm navigating in the dark.

Their first morning at sea dawned with a spectacular blue Asian sky and a gentle, warm breeze. Walt had the helm. George was in the cockpit petting and comforting Gou. The poor dog wasn't quite sure where he was, but he accepted the reassurance of the only guys he trusted. Steve and Paul awoke from their sleep in the bunks below and came on deck. It was 0700h and time for breakfast.

Breakfast was oatmeal—full bowls, and no language barrier this time. Paul started the water boiling and opened the Hop Sing oats box. Since this was the first breakfast out of port, the milk was fresh, and with sugar, cinnamon, and raisins to add to the oatmeal, it was a banquet. Paul thought it was a successful first meal and the rest of the crew agreed. Gou seemed just as happy with his dog food.

Watch change came at 0800h when Steve and Paul took over the helm and checked the sails. They were running with their Genoa jib, main, and mizzen sails. It was the right setting for the wind. Having the correct sails up was important because not enough sail would sacrifice speed and too much sail in a strong wind could lead to the rigging being damaged. Yawls like the *Suzy Wong* are rigged with fore-and-aft sails, the most effective rigging for a modern sailboat. The wind direction hadn't changed; in fact, it had remained constant all night.

The morning was without incident and with each passing hour, the crew was becoming more confident that sailing would turn out to be a breeze. Before they knew it, it was time for lunch. Paul made swiss cheese sandwiches with mayo and mustard on fresh bread. To wash down the meal, the crew had a small amount of fresh water to drink.

The boat's two fifty-gallon freshwater tanks had to be used prudently. During preparations for the voyage, the crew had talked about the possibility of collecting rainwater while at sea, but with Gou shedding dog hair all over the deck, the water could wind up being unpalatable. That plan was quickly abandoned, so they had to be careful at all times never to waste water.

The afternoon continued with smooth sailing. Gou stood up in the bow most of the afternoon just looking out at the sea. He sniffed around, still trying to figure out where he was. The crew changed watch twice more during the day before it was time for dinner.

Early in the evening, just after dinner, in the middle of the South China Sea, a seventy-foot Chinese junk approached the *Suzy Wong*, apparently trying to sell some fish. The junk was large and powered by a diesel engine and sails. The *Suzy Wong* was heading in an approximate course of 190 degrees for Manila, sailing as close to the wind as possible in a light breeze.

Several experienced sailors had warned the Americans about pirates in this area. And now at least twenty Chinese crewmen were peering over the railing of the large junk from a close distance. They were sizing up the smaller boat with seemingly just four guys and a dog. Steve reflected for a moment on his experience on the *Ping Po* in these same waters and recalled their concerns about pirates or thugs from the Chinese mainland. It didn't take much effort to imagine those sailors as brigands with black eye patches, long curved swords, and bejeweled daggers, swarming onto their deck. George was on the helm and ordered all hands on deck. Walt, who was George's watch partner, helped Steve make ready the weapons in case of attack.

The Great Leap Forward in China was in full force. Hong Kong itself had a population comprised of one-third Communist, one-third Nationalist, and the rest any number of political or ideological loyalties. A number of ships, including private boats, had been seized or had disappeared and their crews never heard from again. This rank amateur crew was barely a hundred miles from Mainland China and only on their second day out to sea. Fear seized them and they leapt into position, ready to do what they must to protect their boat and their lives.

When the junk pulled within hailing distance, their weapons were loaded and hidden out of sight in the cockpit, ready for use. Considering that the *Suzy Wong* was a much smaller, slower boat with just four men aboard, the Americans realized they must avoid letting the junk get any closer to them. The Chinese boat's reason for approaching the *Suzy Wong* was unclear, and the language barrier prevented the crew from finding out. With a lack of better options, they had to assume the "pirates" were hostile and not to be taken lightly.

George turned the wheel hard to starboard and, using sail and engine, the *Suzy Wong* managed to head away from the junk. They were on this new course for ten minutes when they saw that the Chinese junk was after them again. This time it got closer and its crew was waving old clothes and making wild gestures that held no meaning for the Americans. The *Suzy Wong's* crew wanted to avoid a confrontation because only a slight nudge could have demolished their boat's lightly constructed hull. The junk looked as if it had been sailing the South China Sea for generations, as the sails were filled with purple patches and held in place by well-worn rigging. The ship's sides were darkened with age and markings, and Chinese characters had been carved into its bow. There appeared to be several registration numbers, showing that it had probably changed hands many times during its history.

The *Suzy Wong* changed course yet again to avoid being crushed or captured. Her distance was now only fifty feet away, far too close for comfort. At this point the crew decided to show their guns to indicate their intention to fight if necessary. The smaller boat again headed at a ninety-degree angle away from the junk. Finally, the distance between the two vessels grew larger, until the would-be pirates slowly turned about and sailed toward China, leaving the *Suzy Wong* to sail on toward its destination. The crew could only guess at the Chinese ship's intentions. Were they pirates? Were they trying to sell fish? Were they friendly? The Americans weren't taking any chances, not on their first full day at sea.

On the third day, there wasn't a ripple on the surface of the water, but the swells were huge. The crew spotted an aircraft carrier with a superstructure at least ten stories above the water. It then simply disappeared out of sight as the carrier rode the backside of a wave. The swells were so large it felt like their boat was climbing up one side of Kilimanjaro and riding down the other. Although they were well off the coast of China and in the open ocean, there were still ships passing in the sea lanes relatively close to land.

Gou looked comical in the swells—like a speed skater making sharp turns. He leaned into and slid away from the center of the boat when he found himself on the downside of a swell. It didn't faze him. He just kept compensating his movements so he never lost his balance. He kept on going round and round the deck. The *Suzy Wong* rode the waves well. In truth, the aircraft carrier probably had a rougher time of it. Swells of this magnitude don't affect a small sailboat, but they can play havoc with a large vessel.

Midshipman Gou sniffs for pirates; South China Sea

The *Suzy Wong* had no electronic navigational equipment and the radio could only transmit an emergency signal and receive shortwave broadcasts. Even with the small transmitter and a few emergency crystals, the crew couldn't have actually contacted anyone in that part of the world. As far as they were concerned, they might as well have been on a distant planet. They couldn't reach anyone and no one could reach them.

They had a sextant to shoot the stars for navigation and a knot log (like a speedometer) to measure the distance traveled through the water. The knot log operated with a small propeller (that drove the log meter). It was tied to the end of a line trailing the boat. On overcast nights, when a celestial position was not possible, they used dead reckoning to calculate their position. That meant calculating the distance covered on the knot log and adding in the effect of any estimated drift. In other words, navigation for *Suzy's* crew was calculated guesswork.

On their third night out, they took a sighting of the stars with the sextant to estimate their position. Their calculations showed they were twenty-five miles inside China, on dry land. This was impossible! At first there were the hurled accusations that the navigator had screwed up, followed by the less volatile expressions of frustration that maybe none of them knew what they were doing. Finally came the even less assuring speculation that maybe the sextant didn't work. In any case, they still didn't know where they were.

So the next day upon sighting a nearby ship, the crew did something that men have never been want to do—they asked for directions! This incredibly technical method of communication involved waving wildly at the other ship and shouting, "Where are we?" It took a quarter of a mile for the passing ship to change its course slightly in order to bring it closer to the *Suzy Wong*. Walt was able to get a good look at the ship and recognized it as an American LST (Landing Ship Tank), the type of ship used during World War II to disgorge tanks. As the ship passed, a crewman on the LST threw a board over the side with a small sealed bottle attached. The bottle held the present position coordinates. Relieved to learn of their correct position, the *Suzy* crew reset their knot log to zero and waved in gratitude as the ship resumed its course.

CHAPTER 16

GALLEY DUTY

Each man had his own area of responsibility and expertise in the day-to-day routine. Walt was in charge of the engine and most mechanical things. George and Steve had the most history with the boat and were designated the master sailors (however ironic that might be, considering their limited sailing experience). Paul was in charge of the food as chef par excellence.

Paul had done a lot of homework about cooking on a boat at sea while in Hong Kong. He had talked to many people who had experience with this fine art. During the voyage, Paul would have to conduct a number of culinary experiments using seawater. He could boil rice in seawater and it turned out fine, but potatoes cooked in seawater quickly turned to a mushy paste. And spaghetti, as it turns out, would also need to be cooked in fresh water.

The boat had just an icebox for refrigeration, so the crew could count on fresh food for only the first three days out from every port because that was how long the ice lasted. The menus were therefore limited, using nonperishable canned goods as often as possible. As ocean-racing sailboats are, by design, often short on storage space, these food items were conveniently stored in the bilge (under the cabin floorboard). From there, the cook could merely lean over and pull out a can that would serve as the start of an evening meal. However, thanks to the flooding incident in Hong Kong and the unlabeled cans, the crew's evening meals were often a surprise. The daily diet saw a lot of dishes made from Spam or tuna, delicacies Steve affectionately called "fart food." The first dinner aboard the *Suzy Wong* was tuna-ghetti.

The crew had acquired its silverware from one of Hong Kong's ship graveyards. Shipwrecking yards cut up old, damaged, or decommissioned ships and then sold off the parts to buyers at bargain prices. Entering one of these yards was an exciting experience, as they held piles of all the things you could imagine finding on an ocean liner: cleats the size of a car, anchor chains large enough to stay the *Queen Mary* in a storm, bed linens, towels, and an abundance of silver-plated flatware. There they acquired flatware at a rock bottom price, along with two well-used sextants.

Jimmy's Kitchen on Hankow Road in Hong Kong made the crew a gift of large oval-shaped plates. Having proper dishes and flatware, of course, meant having to find an easy way to do the dishes every day. The lee side of a boat, which is sheltered from the wind, is the side of the boat where the deck and railing are closer to the water. The men discovered they could lean over the leeside railing to wash their dishes in the seawater. They had to remember to hold each dish tightly because if it slipped out of their hands, it was history.

In addition to planning the meals, the actual act of cooking was a challenge. The stove was fueled by alcohol because the other fuel choices were too messy or posed too great a risk of fire. With compressed gas, there was always the danger of a leak, and leaking gas would settle at the bottom of the boat where any spark might cause an explosion. Gasoline was also a possibility, but it, too, was highly flammable. Finally, they considered using electricity, but the boat didn't have a sufficient power source, so it had to be an alcohol stove.

Unfortunately, as Paul would soon learn, an alcohol stove doesn't produce a lot of heat. It was only a matter of time before they decided to modify the stove to heat the burner initially with alcohol and then switch to pressurized kerosene, which burns hotter. Preheating the burner with alcohol was necessary to keep down the use of kerosene. Too much kerosene would have turned the galley ceiling black.

While building the boat, it was Paul's idea that the galley should have an oven, so the crew had one made to fit on top of the two-burner stove. It was a large brass hood that sat on a thick metal base. However, the oven created a danger—not only of fire, but also of burning someone if he were to bump up against it. Steve quipped, "Storing it takes up the space of a crew member and it can't even take a turn on the helm. Let's lose it." It was agreed, somewhere in the South China Sea, that the oven attachment was a bad idea, so it was tossed overboard. Without an oven, Paul had to become more creative and fry the food that could no longer be baked. Despite this inconvenience, everyone agreed the food was pretty remarkable for an ocean crossing with a galley that was makeshift at best.

Early on they all agreed that whoever cooked a meal would be exempt from doing the dishes. Oftentimes, however, it turned out that the designated dishwasher was busy doing something else, leaving Paul to do the cooking *and* the cleaning. After a few days of being left with a mess, an overworked Paul mutinied; he dirtied all the dishes and walked out, refusing any more galley duty. He had made his point. After that, the crew designated a "Hell Day" for each member every fourth day, giving Paul a break from the galley while one other crew member did all the cooking *and* cleaning. This system quickly solved the problem of inequitable kitchen duty.

Chapter 17

Sink or Swim

Paul was most comfortable around the galley and least comfortable on deck. In part, this was because he didn't know how to swim. The rest of the crew was concerned about this and decided they needed to teach Paul to swim—or, at the very least, keep him from drowning.

Paul was given his first swimming lesson not in a pool where his feet could touch bottom, but in the South China Sea, where the bottom was two thousand feet below him. It was fortunate that George Todd had been an All-American swimmer in high school and that Steve and Walt were also good swimmers. Consequently, Paul had good teachers. They tied a rope around his waist and into the ocean he jumped. Paul struggled to the surface and paddled back and forth from the stern to the bow. Paul's first swimming lesson lasted only twenty minutes and he was exhausted. His trainers were all on deck shouting to encourage him while he struggled to keep his head above water. No one swam beside him because that was what the rope was for, to keep him safely attached to the boat at all times. He dog-paddled to the bow of the boat and back three times and then signaled to come aboard.

Paul remarked that his father had learned to swim in the Atlantic off the Azore Islands when he was a boy. The unsympathetic sailors on deck laughed at the thought of Paul's father seeing his son with a rope tied around his waist as he struggled to swim. Eventually, Paul learned to dog paddle and float, but he never did become a decent swimmer.

The South China Sea is known for violent typhoons and sudden changes of weather. Here is where the inexperienced sailors were just plain lucky. Since leaving Hong Kong, the weather had been forgiving—enabling them time to learn how to operate their new vessel. Outside of getting lost and encountering suspected pirates, the journey had passed without incident.

The *Suzy Wong* sailed into sight of Luzon in the Philippines on March 12, 1960. At 1530h, the crew sighted the US Navy radio facility, San Miguel, followed five hours later by the sighting of the US Naval Base at Subic Bay. Very early the next morning, they passed the beacon on Corregidor Island that marked the entrance into Manila Bay. Due to its location at the mouth of the Bay, the Island of Corregidor was used as a point of defense for the city of Manila thirty miles to the east. This was also the location where General Douglas McArthur made his famous, well-documented landing, fulfilling his pledge to return to liberate the Philippines.

Hitting fifteen to twenty-knot winds and heavy swells, the *Suzy Wong* commenced tacking toward her destination. Fourteen hours later, Commander Skidmore in his sloop, the *Ping Po*, met the *Suzy Wong* and escorted her to Sangley Point. They had successfully arrived at their first port of call.

As far as the crew knew, Gou had never relieved himself on board during the first leg of the voyage. The reason for his restraint wasn't modesty, but rather uncertainty as to what to do and how to do it on a heaving, lurching, constantly moving deck. The moment the boat docked at Sangley Point, with relief in sight, Gou jumped off the boat so fast he missed the dock. Paddling through the water, the dog came dangerously close to being crushed between the boat and the dock. He scrambled to dry ground and promptly peed on the first palm tree in sight.

The *Suzy Wong's* arrival in the Philippines was big news. On March 13 the boat sailed directly to the Sangley Point Naval Base. Being familiar with the base because they had lived there, the Americans overlooked the requirement to register with Philippine Customs. As freshman sailors, and as this was their first port of call, they forgot about this rather serious detail. The crew of the *Suzy Wong* was immediately instructed to hightail it across Manila Bay to a commercial dock in Manila where their boat would be registered with the authorities.

Owing to this infraction, the Philippines Immigration Department was annoyed. The boat and the crew were quarantined. The *Suzy Wong* was berthed between two large freighters whose decks were higher than *Suzy's* 55-foot mast.

The Americans remained in quarantine for two days, after which they were rescued from their boredom by the likely entreaties of Commander Skidmore and the US Navy. Even with all the hassle, the crew saw their safe arrival at Sangley Point as a positive sign that luck was on their side.

Their luck continued a few days later when they met the owner of a rope manufacturing company near Manila who invited them to tour his factory. Honored that the now-famous *Suzy Wong* crew would pay him a visit, he made a special coil of yacht rope. This rope was made from a higher quality fiber and had a different weave than the usual Manila rope, making it easier on your hands. Though their host mispronounced "yacht" to sound like "yatch," the crew was very appreciative of the gift.

Having made it through the first leg of their journey unscathed, the crew relaxed and enjoyed some downtime. During their ten days in Manila, they had the sextant checked and repaired; Walt, George, and Steve visited friends; Paul didn't have to cook; and Gou had a much easier time doing his business watering the local plant life.

CHAPTER 18

THE PHILIPPINES

As a reservist, Walter had to fulfill a two-week naval reserve commitment every year. He had hoped to meet this requirement when the *Suzy Wong* docked in Manila, and the navy did indeed allow him to do so. He would be working with a master chief quartermaster, a navigation specialist. Unfortunately, this meant that Walter would need to stay in Manila for a bit longer than the crew intended to stay. So the *Suzy Wong* would proceed on its way without Walt for a brief time, with a plan to catch up with him later.

This gave Steve a chance to invite one of his naval officer buddies, Lou Cherichetti from Sangley, to take Walt's place on the next leg of the trip. Steve knew Lou because the two of them had taken a number of adventures together on the island of Luzon during their tours of duty at Sangley. Lou had been aware of the *Suzy Wong* endeavor almost from the beginning, even visiting Hong Kong during the boat's construction. Steve had wanted him to be a permanent crew member, but his military commitment didn't allow for that. Now, however, the timing was right, and Lou could fill the empty spot and crew to their next port of call.

At 1650h on March 23, the *Suzy Wong* departed Manila with George, Steve, Paul, Gou, and new crew member, Lou. They headed west out of Manila Bay, past Corregidor Island, and then south, sailing toward Palawan, the southwestern-most island in the Philippines. Their destination was the US Coast Guard Loran Station at Trumpitao Point on Palawan. The estimated sailing time would be five days.

After seeing Gou's reluctance to relieve himself on board, George tossed the palm tree overboard. It hadn't worked because Gou had no idea why it was there. George decided it was time to teach the dog how to do his business on deck. He took a gunny sack up forward, dropped his pants, and proceeded to defecate on the sack to demonstrate to Gou what he needed to do. Gou merely tilted his head to the side to signal his confusion. The lesson didn't take immediately, but eventually Gou learned from this example and did it in his own way. He would wait until the sails were down and then do his business on the most forward sail.

On the way to Palawan, a school of dolphins played alongside the boat, weaving intricate patterns at the bow. It seemed like a game for them. To watch them at close range was fascinating for the crew because the dolphins swam as a unit, intuitively knowing exactly what the others were doing. Gou was even more intrigued. He stood on the bow watching them for hours, perhaps hoping for potential playmates.

Trumpitao Point was a small military base whose short and narrow grass landing strip was carved out of the dense jungle. The Coast Guard operated the base as a Loran navigation outpost, providing signals to help ships and aircraft find their position while traversing that part of Southeast Asia. This is where Walter would eventually rendezvous with the crew upon finishing his reserve duty in Manila.

Paul and Steve befriended a slightly built local nicknamed Peanuts, who had been a military guide to the US Army during World War II. His Pidgin English was fairly good, so they could understand what he said. He offered to take them several miles upriver one day in a small Philippine banca boat. Before setting out, they had to do some bailing, as it had rained the night before. There may have been a few small leaks in his boat as well.

Paul and Peanuts paddle up jungle river; Palawan, Philippines

The lush greenery of the jungle lined both sides of the river. At a wide place in the river they encountered a bunch of boys having a raucous time as they played with water buffaloes. Splashing about in the water, the boys jumped bareback on a buffalo and rode the frightened animal to the shore. After returning, Peanuts informed Paul and Steve that there were crocodiles in that river. Surprisingly, that fact didn't seem to be a concern to the boys.

The homes along the path to the river were primitive little dwellings that looked like they'd topple into the water if anyone sneezed too hard. They were built of bamboo, had thatched roofs, and stood elevated on stilts. Steve remarked to Paul, "If by chance you were to drop a pencil, it would go straight through the bamboo floor and you'd need to go outside to pick it up."

Palawan was a primitive place where some of the children were unable to go to school because they didn't have clothes to wear. Paul had a soft heart when it came to kids, so he arranged for his brother and sister-in-law (Bert and Edith) to send boxes of clothes for the children, organized through their children's school and the PTA. The crew arranged for the local Coast Guard station to receive the goods, and shipping costs were low.

The natives who received the clothing would later write a letter to Edith, thanking her for her generosity. The letter also informed her of how much the Palawan natives had appreciated *Suzy Wong's* visit, and they assured her they had kept an eye out to protect the crew from pirates. Hearing about the pirates, Edith immediately wrote a letter to Paul imploring him to abandon the trip and come home! But, of course, he didn't.

Paul enjoyed his time in Palawan, but then he always had a good time wherever he was. He liked to entertain his newfound friends with a few card tricks he had mastered while in the military. He usually traveled with a deck or two in his pocket and could almost always find an opportunity to pull them out. They were great icebreakers, especially when language barriers might have otherwise led to awkward smiles and long silences. Palawan was no exception. Soon the villagers were crowded around Paul, chatting and laughing in amazement. They thought he was some sort of deity the way he could identify the particular cards they held in their hands.

After just three days on Palawan, it was time to set sail again. The navy commander in Manila had given Walt an early discharge from his reserve duty and he found a Coast Guard pilot willing to fly him from Manila to Trumpitao Point on Palawan. Walt landed and rejoined the crew, while Lou took the return flight back to Manila. On April 1 at 1625h, the log recorded, "Up anchor & underway from Trumpitao bound for Jesselton, Borneo."

The boat sailed down the long, jagged western coastline of Palawan, which was dotted with hundreds of monolithic limestone formations, creating an obstacle course along its entire length. Closer to land, the view was a beautiful dreamscape of islands and rounded mounds peeking above the water's surface, all covered in dense greenery. The boat moved farther out to sea to ply a straighter course, and from that vantage point the morning mist made the islands look like shrouded sentinels keeping watch over the coast.

Chapter 19

Leading a Celebrity Life

Early in the morning on April 4, the crew sighted the coast of Borneo. By lunchtime they had tied up to a dock in Jesselton. Word had arrived ahead of them, thanks to publicist Irving Hoffman in Hong Kong, elevating their status to that of celebrity. There were scarce few modern visiting sailboats arriving in Jesselton, so they were easy to spot. The first invitation came almost immediately from the president of the leading British bank in the form of a dinner invitation. While at dinner, the crew learned some of the history of that part of Borneo, which they found fascinating.

The British North Borneo Company (BNBC) came to Borneo in 1898 and was established in a small fishing village called Api-Api. They designated this harbor port town as the terminus for the North Borneo Railway. The town was later renamed Jesselton after Sir Charles Jessel who, at that time, was BNBC's vice chairman. Jesselton traded many products such as lumber, rubber, honey and wax throughout the British Empire until World War II, when most of the buildings were destroyed to prevent them from falling into the hands of the Japanese.

After the war, the BNBC returned to administer Jesselton,

Passionate Paul writes ladylove Mary; Jesselton, Borneo

but they couldn't afford the enormous costs of reconstructing the town. Control of Jesselton was turned over to the British Crown in 1946, and the new colonial government reestablished it as the capital of North Borneo. British influence was still very much apparent in 1960 when the crew of the *Suzy Wong* docked there.

Paul had begun corresponding with Mary DeForest, the girl he met in Hong Kong on the Star Ferry. By this time she had been transferred to the American Embassy in Madrid, Spain.

The first morning after their arrival in North Borneo, Paul wrote:

> Downtown Jesselton is just beginning to move. It's 6:30 a.m. and like in any other city, things are starting to whip into shape for the day. Steve and I got up this morning to write letters and get them to the post office before 8:00 a.m., which is the last airmail for two days. We are on our way to Brunei, North Borneo and decided to stop in Jesselton along the way. We took care of customs and immigration yesterday, soon after our arrival. Then one of the top officials invited us to the Yacht Club for a drink. We wound up having dinner at the largest residence in Jesselton, owned by the president of the bank. Jesselton has a population of approximately 12,000 and is like a valley town in California. It is the cleanest city we have been in, and the beauty is something to see. Tomorrow the bank president's wife, who has a private railway car, is going to take us into the interior of the country. What a deal. Almost sounds like make-believe.

The next day the crew rode a single-car train toward the nearly 14,000-foot Mount Kinabalu to the town of Penampang to meet some local officials. There was no particular reason for meeting the officials, but it gave the crew an excuse to see the countryside. The sailors were being treated like celebrities now and had a special letter of introduction. None of them ever thought of themselves as celebrities, but arriving by their beautiful boat from a far-off land was the object of some attention and they were beginning to get used to their new status.

Paul welcoming crewmates aboard BNBC's minicar; Jesselton, Borneo

The train car was a strange-looking contraption, more like a large enclosed Jeep with wheels made for railroad tracks. The bank president's wife routinely volunteered at a tuberculosis sanatorium partway to their destination, so she accompanied the new arrivals for a portion of their trip. When she disembarked at her stop, she hopped on a donkey and rode out of sight into the dense jungle underbrush. Later that day, she reappeared at the side of the tracks where she had left them and together they enjoyed their return trip to Jesselton.

That evening, one of their new friends asked the crew if they had seen the flying foxes. The Americans had never heard of them, but that night they learned that flying foxes are actually enormous bats—the largest in the world, with a wingspan of up to seven feet. Being fruit bats, they feed only on nectar, blossoms, pollen, and fruit, limiting the environs in which they can thrive. They do not have sonar and must use scent and sight to locate their food. At dusk each evening, the bats leave their daytime perches in the trees or under the rock overhangs and take to the air. Thousands of them fly from one side of the bay to the other to feed.

The crew stepped outdoors to watch this daily spectacle. The phenomenon of the sky darkening as the swarming mass of bats partly obscured the last dwindling light of the setting sun was truly incredible to the Americans. They had seen nothing quite like this before.

Shortly before their arrival in Jesselton, the boat's exhaust system developed a leak. Steve in particular, and Paul to a lesser degree, had a difficult time in the cabin with the foul-smelling fumes from the damaged exhaust system. Steve was prone to seasickness and the fumes from the engine were difficult for him to tolerate. The problem was caused by the chemical reaction of salt seawater (which ran through the engine) mixing with diesel engine gases. This resulted in the formation of sulfuric acid, which had a devastatingly corrosive effect on the jacketed exhaust system and a nauseating effect on the sailors working below deck.

Steve and Paul had to do something about it. They wanted George and Walt to take action and fix the problem, but that didn't seem to be on their agenda. In their frustration and alone on the boat, Steve and Paul took matters into their own hands. They unbolted and ripped out the exhaust system. When Walt and George returned, they were predictably furious. It was their responsibility to make sure *Suzy's* mechanical systems worked properly and this was not the way to do it.

Repairs had to be made before they could depart Jesselton. It was not an easy task, as the exhaust pipe looked strangely like a labyrinthine section of human intestines. It had several large bends designed to prevent water from backing into the engine, and it was jacketed. (That is, it had a pipe within a pipe so water could circulate around the hot exhaust pipe inside the confines of the boat.) It would be difficult to find the proper replacement parts to match its odd, twisting shape. This took a while, so their departure was delayed.

With help from a nearby metal shop, Walt and George were able to work their usual magic on the repairs, but they made no secret of their displeasure at what they considered to be an impetuous act by Paul and Steve. This disagreement became a major argument, almost leading to a fistfight. It was the first serious problem to temporarily fracture the crew's harmony. The mood among them was frosty for a brief period, but their ability to work together as a team was absolutely imperative, especially in potentially life-threatening situations, so all was forgiven after a while and the incident was mostly forgotten by the time they set sail again.

CHAPTER 20

GUESTS OF THE SULTAN OF BRUNEI

On April 7 the *Suzy Wong* sailed out of Jesselton along the northern coast of Borneo. The crew had an impressive view of the 13,435-foot high Mount Kinabalu towering over the island in the distance. It is one of the tallest mountains in Southeast Asia. On this sunny day with calm seas, the *Suzy Wong* glided silently and effortlessly alongside the jungle-laden coastline. The exhaust system was fixed, and the small rupture in relations between members of *Suzy's* crew seemed to have been mended as well. Paul and Steve had achieved their purpose and could once again breathe easily inside the cabin with the engine running.

The boat sailed to Labuan Island, one of a small cluster of islands just five miles off the coast. It was a good-sized island, but flat with a slight undulation to its contours. It looked like any other island in Southeast Asia—covered in dense foliage in the deepest shades of jungle green. Labuan did not provide much in the way of unique beauty, but it did have a harbor in the town of Victoria where the *Suzy Wong* could dock for the night.

Early the next morning the boat shoved off from Victoria Harbor. The April 8 log entry stated, "The weather is fair with no wind…at 1010 hours passed abeam Sapo Point & entered Brunei River." The crew motored the boat ten miles up the Brunei River to the capital, Bandar Seri Begawan, tying up at the public pier by mid-afternoon. The Americans had arrived in the Sultanate of Brunei.

Thanks again to Hoffman, all of Brunei had heard about the voyage of the *Suzy Wong*. On the day of *Suzy's* arrival, an article appeared in the *North Borneo News and Sabah Times*. The front-page headline read "*Suzy Wong* in Jesselton" with a cover photo of Walt, Paul, Steve, George, and Gou posing nicely for the camera.

As a result of the publicity, Omar Ali Saifuddin, Sultan of Brunei, sent the Americans a request to come aboard their boat. Paul quickly wrote an invitation and had it hand-delivered to the royal palace. Unfortunately, a subsequent emergency meeting of the States of North Borneo required the Sultan's presence elsewhere. So the Sultan invited the crew to come and visit his palace instead. In typical American fashion, *Suzy's* sailors arrived at the elegant palace casually dressed in shorts and sneakers. They were graciously escorted through the palace's public rooms, which looked to them like the elaborate, ornate ballrooms found in fancy hotels.

Official guests of Sultan Omar Ali Saifuddin; Brunei, Borneo

The Sultan also gave them a formal invitation to visit the magnificent mosque, which was named after him. The crew had first glimpsed it when they motored up the river—its 160-foot-high golden dome gleaming in the afternoon sun and rising above the treetops. Only just completed in 1958, the Taj Mahal–like mosque was already developing a reputation as one of the most magnificent structures in the world.

A visit to the mosque was a special honor, as non-Muslims were not generally allowed to go inside such a Muslim holy place. The sailors marveled at the exquisite Islamic architecture, magnificent mosaics, stained-glass windows, and rich details in its arches, domes, and columns. The mosque was made of marble from Italy and granite from Shanghai and featured chandeliers from England. All these elements were elegantly incorporated to make it Brunei's most unforgettable and cherished building.

Brunei was a country of great wealth from oil revenue, and the benevolent Sultan provided things he believed his people wanted and needed: he established basic education throughout his country; he improved the country's communication system and raised the quality of medical and health services; he built roads and provided electricity and water to all his people; and he made outboard motors available for every small boat in Brunei. The constant buzz of all the outboards was deafening.

The crew noticed one curious feature in Brunei. Although the country was spending money building new housing and bringing basic modern conveniences to its people, rickety wooden structures on stilts overhung the river. They weren't fancy houses taking advantage of the view on pricey waterfront property; they were dilapidated shacks originally built by pirates. To be over the river was a necessity for their original occupants. The river provided ease of sanitation as well as a route for quick exits to escape the authorities. It seemed odd to the crew that the Sultan's program to rapidly modernize and beautify the city allowed these eyesores to remain.

Former pirate shacks dominate Brunei River waterfront; Borneo

On their second day in Brunei, the crew moved their boat to the Royal Brunei Yacht Club. Due to the press coverage of their adventure, people presumed the American crew to be experts in international sailing. George, Walt, Paul, and Steve knew they weren't; however, they accepted an invitation to compete in one of the Yacht Club's weekend sailing regattas.

Given boats with which to compete, the Americans were split up into two teams—Paul and George, and Steve and Walt. The boats were small, barely twelve feet long, with a centerboard. They were the right kind of craft for a river. George was busy on board getting the boat ready to race. Finally, he called Paul to step aboard. Paul, being proportionally stout and used to stepping aboard the much larger *Suzy Wong*, grabbed the mast at head height and swung his body hoping to land on deck. Unfortunately, this small boat had a high center of gravity and only a centerboard for ballast. The boat instantly capsized, tossing both George and Paul into the river and out of the race—much to the delight of everyone watching.

CHAPTER 21

OFF COURSE

The log for April 11, 1960, at 0635h read, "Departed Brunei bound for Singapore, Malaya with four crewmen aboard." This would be the crew's biggest challenge, as they were about to sail the longest leg of their journey thus far. The sail to Singapore would require a full week of continuous sailing, give or take a few days.

On April 12 the boat passed through a squall line. The motion of the boat was intense and Paul got thrown about the cabin, breaking a window when he fell against it. Two days later the crew sailed into another heavy rainstorm. The boat suffered no additional damage and the men enjoyed a thorough drenching. It was a blessing, really. They had been sweltering in the relentless heat and humidity of the South China Sea. Not only did the rain cool them off, it washed away some of the stench from their sweaty bodies.

Suzy Wong leaving Borneo—destination Singapore

On April 15 the crew motored all day because there was little wind to fill the sails. The boat chugged along at about four knots with its small Stuart Turner diesel engine. The heat and constant chugging of the engine made the days and nights seem endless. The guys had to keep reminding themselves that this was supposed to be a fun adventure. They just wanted this leg of the trip to come to an end as soon as possible.

Then, at 0200h on the morning of April 16, the *Suzy Wong* had a near disaster. Paul and Steve were on watch, with Paul at the helm and Steve dozing on the cockpit cushions next to him. Paul was faced with a new situation and didn't know what to do, so he woke Steve saying, "I see a red and green light coming toward us. What should I do?" Half in a slumber, Steve replied, "Favor green, Paul." Then he stretched out and went to sleep again within seconds.

A few minutes later, Paul tugged Steve's leg wildly. When Steve opened his eyes, all he could see was the bow of a ship coming directly at their small forty-one-foot boat. Together, they spun the wheel to port in order to change course. *Suzy's* response was immediate. The large ship kept coming and coming until it was nearly on top of them. The small sailboat turned in place like a toy top and succeeded in getting out of the way just in the nick of time! Paul and Steve stood there while a huge freighter slid by in the dark, missing them with only a few feet to spare.

The bow wave of the freighter splashed over the *Suzy Wong*, completely drenching George and Walt who were sound asleep on the forward deck. *Suzy* was a solid small vessel made of wood with two and a half tons of lead attached to her underside to keep her upright in heavy seas. However, had that large freighter hit her, she would have shattered, possibly killing everyone on board before sinking without a trace.

The lesson learned from this incident was that knowing the international navigational rules of the sea is extremely important. The crew escaped unharmed, but Paul couldn't help feeling that his lack of sailing experience revealed itself at the helm that night.

They surmised that no one had been on the bridge of the freighter to see them. The freighter was off the sea lanes and not too concerned about spotting another boat because the waters of Borneo are not heavily traveled. In the wake of this almost-disastrous incident, the crew decided that at their next port they would acquire an automotive headlight and hook it up to the boat's battery. The plan was to have this light illuminate their large white sail at night, making it easier for other ships to spot them in the darkness.

As a habit, the crew trailed a fishing line with the hopes of catching an evening's meal. One of the many lessons they learned was that mid-ocean fishing was practically pointless. It wasn't until they reached shoaling waters that they had any luck at all. Many times their trailing fishing line would become entangled with the trailing knot log, necessitating the tedious task of untangling the two lines.

One day the water around the boat was swarming with sea snakes. The guys couldn't believe how many there were—hundreds of thousands, maybe millions—as far as the eye could see in every direction. Just for fun, and to relieve the tedium of the long voyage, they started harassing the thrashing snakes. Paul pounded them with the boat hook. George thought it was a good time to have target practice with his pistol. Gou took in the action with his usual silent stare. They had no idea the snakes were poisonous. It was a good thing the crew didn't catch any fish for food, as they later learned that many of the fish eat the snakes and become poisonous themselves.

After passing through the sea snakes, the *Suzy Wong* was still about two days out from Singapore, far from any land mass. In the middle of the night, they began looking for a navigational light on the horizon marking a hazard as well as providing them with a positive navigational fix. (Navigational lights are coordinated all over the world, each having a unique signal comprised of long and short flashes displayed in a measurable time interval.) As expected, the light appeared, but it was sending the wrong signal according to their chart. They timed the signal flashes again very carefully and, sure enough, the signal didn't agree with their chart. Yet it appeared in the expected location.

Their first assumption was that the marker was incorrect and needed to be reported. Walt was the cautious member of the crew and insisted that they had better hold up in order to obtain a celestial fix

Suzy's armaments in action,
George and Paul; South China Sea

before proceeding. The moon was shining and they could make out the horizon and some identifiable stars. Meanwhile, they sailed in a triangular pattern to hold their position. It was after midnight when they took their reading of the stars. Then Walter went to work figuring out where they were by making his navigational calculations, a process that took several hours to complete.

To their dismay, they discovered that they were more than a hundred miles south of their intended course. Had they proceeded, they would surely have run aground on a reef outcropping some five miles ahead. Here is where caution and common sense prevailed, saving the crew from certain disaster, if not death. This was the second near-disaster in almost as many days. It served to remind the crew to be more careful with their navigational calculations and to remain vigilant about their location at all times.

Early on the morning of April 19, the crew sighted the Horseborough Lighthouse, marking the center of the Singapore Straits. The log recorded that at 1535h they had, "Entered Singapore Harbor." An hour later the boat had cleared entry with customs and health officials, finally dropping anchor at the Royal Singapore Yacht Club Basin.

In a letter to Mary dated April 19, Paul wrote:

> The trip from Brunei was rather slow as the winds were from light to dead. We had to motor-sail much of the way. We are anchored next to the Royal Singapore Yacht Club and sitting on the Club's veranda. It is a most impressive sight. It's dusk, and the lights of the ships in the harbor are now visible. I can count thirty-four ocean-going liners and cargo ships. All this, with a background of clouds and the sun's reflection on the water, is enough to make one stop and think of how beautiful nature can be.

The Yacht Club warmly welcomed the *Suzy* crew as honorary members. After their arduous passage across the South China Sea, they needed a little R & R and gratefully accepted the Club's warm hospitality. The crew had no idea how long they would stay in Singapore. They were more concerned with having a good time in the ports they visited than keeping to a strict timetable.

Chapter 22

A Steal in Singapore

Singapore was a joy. This city seemed even more exotic to the Americans than Hong Kong had been when they first began their journey. Ancient Chinese accounts dating as far back as the third century described Singapore as an "island at the end of a peninsula." The city-island began to take a place of importance in the world during the early nineteenth century when British statesman Sir Thomas Raffles realized the potential of this up-and-coming trading post situated at the center of the major sea route through Asia. He signed a treaty in 1819 with Sultan Hussein Shah, and in 1824 the city became a British colony, as it had remained when the *Suzy Wong* arrived there.

In 1960 Singapore was a true melting pot where the cultures and histories of different countries had merged over the centuries and yet retained their individual identities. The population was comprised of people from the Malay Kingdom, China, East Pakistan, India, and Thailand, as well as expatriates and workers from the United States and Europe. One could literally see, hear, and taste some vestige of each culture in the vibrant hues and bold patterns of clothing worn by people in the streets, in the music heard emanating from clubs, and on the tables of countless eateries and restaurants. Singapore was vibrant and alive.

Despite the overwhelming distractions of great food, drink, music, and beautiful women, the crew had plenty of practical things to keep them busy in Singapore. The boat needed serious maintenance: the plumbing had to be revamped because the sink wouldn't drain when the boat was sailing on a starboard tack, the fuel tank needed filling, and then there was the matter of the broken window.

The crew's contacts in Singapore were a couple of guys named Chick Parsons and Pete Grimm. They owned the Luzon Stevedoring Company, which operated in the Philippines and elsewhere in Asia. When Paul first met Chick and Pete in Manila, they offered to help if ever the *Suzy Wong* needed it. Paul had an "in" with Pete Grimm as well; he had gone to junior high and high school in Palo Alto with

Grimms' daughter, Ethel. Paul remembered that Ethel was extremely attractive, having been voted May Queen at school. He also remembered that she didn't want to have anything to do with him back then. Ethel's disinterest, however, didn't stop Paul from making a connection with her father. Any contact was a good one, no matter what the circumstances.

As soon as they docked in Singapore, Paul telephoned the Luzon Stevedoring office and told the manager that the *Suzy Wong* had just arrived and was in need of assistance. Walt and Steve reminded Paul over and over, "You'd better be sure to get a full estimate of the costs before agreeing to anything," because they were low on funds. Despite this, a full-sized seagoing tugboat from the Luzon Stevedoring Company entered the Yacht Club harbor, churning up waves and commotion and chugging toward the *Suzy Wong*. The commodore of the Yacht Club was flabbergasted, flapping his arms and sputtering about such totally unacceptable behavior.

The tug remained calmly beside the *Suzy Wong* and filled her tank with diesel fuel. The Luzon Company workers eliminated the drain problem by installing an auxiliary hand-pump. They replaced the broken window, and even did some touch-up varnishing. When Paul asked for the bill, the Luzon Company manager said, "That will be thirty-three dollars, please."

Paul said, "Wait a minute. The fuel alone cost more than that."

"Don't worry. I charged that to the Russian freighter over there."

"What about the plumbing and the window?" Paul asked.

The manager replied, "I charged that to the American President Shipping Line."

Paul couldn't resist, so he asked, "Well, then, what are we paying for?"

He said, "Just the labor. I couldn't charge the labor to anyone else because it's done on a time-clock."

Then Paul said, "Pete Grimm said we could pay with a check. May I write you a personal check?"

"Yes, of course."

So Paul wrote out a check.

"Would that be a US bank check?"

"Yes," said Paul.

"Well, the thirty-three is in Malay currency. In US dollars it comes to eleven."

Paul tore up the first check and wrote another personal check for the correct amount. He couldn't remember the manager's name, maybe never knew it, but he felt an instant camaraderie because in chatting he learned that both of them had been rugby players. As the tug pulled away, Paul could see the manager standing on the bridge of his boat. Paul waved in gratitude. Repairs, fuel, and labor had proved a steal in Singapore!

The H.M.S. *Melbourne* happened to be anchored in Singapore at the same time as the *Suzy Wong*. The *Melbourne* was the one and only aircraft carrier of the Australian Navy. News traveled fast among sailors who brought stories from other ports of call and shared them with sailors, who in turn had their own tales to tell. In this way, the Americans heard that several Aussie Navy mates from the *Melbourne* had recently visited the American Embassy in the Philippines and had swiped a souvenir—a framed picture of President Eisenhower. The crew of the *Suzy Wong* decided to return the favor, if they could.

As *Suzy Wong* celebrities, the Americans were invited to come aboard the *Melbourne* aircraft carrier. As they approached the carrier, they kept their eyes open for something to swipe from the Aussies. They noticed two huge symbolic life rings decorating the fantail of the carrier, proudly imprinted with "H.M.S. *Melbourne*." The Aussies were eager to hear about the *Suzy Wong*'s voyage and to know if there was anything they could do to help out. The Americans decided they could use a lanyard and some waxed line, which their new *Melbourne* mates were happy to provide.

With the help of several Australian aviators, the Americans managed to divert the attention of the duty sailors and lower one of the large Aussie life rings over the side of the carrier and down many feet to the water below, using the waxed line they had just acquired. After taking their leave with profuse thanks for the gracious hospitality of their Aussie hosts, the *Suzy* crew climbed aboard a water taxi and cast off. They directed the taxi to pull alongside the opposite side of the carrier, where they retrieved the stolen five-foot-wide life ring. They headed back to their boat and hoisted the life ring high up the mast. It was theirs now!

At roughly 0400h the next morning, several naval aviators from the H.M.S. *Melbourne* paid the Americans a visit, waking them from a deep sleep. Because the aviators were in on the theft, they had been threatened with court-martial if they didn't collect the life ring and return it to the aircraft carrier. Hearing this, the Americans had a change of heart and relinquished the prize to the Aussies. They didn't get to keep their souvenir, but George, Walt, Paul, and Steve felt that they had at least gotten a small measure of revenge.

The crew received their first letter from Irving Hoffman at the American Embassy in Singapore. Filming of *The World of Suzie Wong* was almost complete and he was soon to leave Hong Kong for home. Hoffman gave the guys his home address so they could stay in touch, writing briefly, "Dear Paul...I will be in New York soon. How's your journey going? Best to you and the boys. Sincerely, Irving."

During their stay in Singapore, *Suzy* was joined by two new crew members. The first sailor was J.D. Malone, who they had originally met in Hong Kong. J.D. thought their plan to sail around the world sounded like a great adventure. He arranged to pay the Americans so that he could come aboard as a working crew member. He was an amiable guy who got along with everybody, so he was a welcome addition. However, by virtue of his not having been with the group from the very beginning, J.D. would always be something of a fifth wheel.

The second new sailor added in Singapore was Blackie Blackburn, a ham radio operator who brought his shortwave radio equipment on board. He was an officer in the American Embassy in Manila at the time when George and Steve were both serving tours of duty at Sangley Point. Blackie had also served alongside Steve as a crew member on Commander Skidmore's inaugural voyage of the *Ping Po* sloop. When the *Suzy Wong* adventure began taking shape, Blackie expressed an interest in joining the crew for at least one leg of the voyage.

The crew stayed on in Singapore for a while longer. The length of time they remained in any one port depended on two factors: how much fun they were having, and their need to press on to cross the Indian Ocean before the onset of the monsoon. On April 28, they determined that it was time to leave Singapore. The *Suzy Wong* departed its anchorage from the Royal Singapore Yacht Club at 1825h and set sail for Penang, Malaysia with six guys and Gou.

Chapter 23

Straits of Malacca

The Strait of Malacca leading to the island of Penang was a narrow 500-mile waterway between the Malayan peninsula and the Indonesian island of Sumatra. Economically and strategically, it was one of the world's most important sea lanes connecting Asia to the Western world. In one spot, close to Singapore, the Strait was only a little over a mile wide, making it one of the world's most strategic choke points. Going through this point was a bit nerve wracking because they were so close to shore. It was easy to imagine being attacked from land. Then again, there was a constant threat of attack from the water; almost any commercial boat could have overtaken the *Suzy Wong*. Their only chance for survival against an assault was their hodgepodge arsenal of weapons.

On April 30 the *Suzy Wong* was sailing up the Straits of Malacca with fair winds and a clear blue sky when suddenly, low on the horizon, two jet aircrafts appeared, coming directly toward the boat. The jets flew so close overhead that the crew could smell the jet fuel from the engines. It was at this point that someone remembered that the pilots from the Australian carrier, the H.M.S. *Melbourne*, had said they would check up on *Suzy* as she sailed north from Singapore. After several low passes, the jets disappeared, only to return several hours later for more low flyovers. Contrary to their worst imaginations, the passage up the Malacca Straits was mostly uneventful. Rather than being attacked, the *Suzy Wong* was carefully protected.

With ham radio operator Blackie on board, everyone got the radio bug. Blackie really knew his stuff, including Morse code. The *Suzy Wong* crew was in the middle of nowhere and got to use Blackie's equipment to communicate with other ham operators half a world away. The guys took turns at the radio, spending hours talking to people in Russia, England, Kenya, Norway, Manila, Singapore, Hong Kong, and the United States. On several occasions, the crew asked the operators to forward messages to their families and friends.

Blackie was a peanut butter freak. He wanted peanut butter at every meal, so he made sure there was plenty of it in stock before leaving Singapore. He proved to be a real character and a delightful guest to have on board. The crew knew that it would not be easy to say goodbye to Blackie Blackburn and his fine radio equipment.

The men arrived in Penang on May 1, 1960. They were directed to a ship chandler, a person whose business it is to sell supplies to major ships. The chandler came to the boat, efficiently handled the *Suzy Wong*'s order, and, when business was finished, asked, "Have you seen the temples in Penang?" They had not, so after Blackie disembarked to return to Manila, the four original crew and J.D. went on a guided tour of several Penang temples.

One temple the crew visited had a sign in front reading "Snake Temple" in English. Upon entering the snake temple, the Americans were greeted by the dull haze of burning incense. Paul's first impression was that hundreds of large curved candlesticks had been thrown about on the floor. On closer inspection, however, those candlesticks were moving! The altar of the temple was literally crawling with hundreds of pit vipers.

It was believed that the incense smoke rendered the vipers lethargic and, therefore, harmless. The monks, nonetheless, had removed the venom from the snakes as an extra safety precaution. The snakes still had their fangs, so the guys were warned against picking them up for snapshots. "No problem there," they thought. Having just learned in Singapore that their last encounter with snakes could have killed them, the four men quickly took in the sight and then calmly backed out of the temple.

Meanwhile, Irving Hoffman was making international phone calls to each port of call that the *Suzy Wong* intended to visit. He usually had no idea of the boat's arrival date, so local reporters would stroll their piers every day just to make sure they wouldn't miss the *Suzy Wong*.

Paul wrote to Mary on May 4:

I have been on the go ever since we arrived. It's the publicity for Paramount that has kept me busy. The results, however, have been well worthwhile. We got big write-ups in the two English papers, three leading Chinese papers, and the local Arabic paper. I'll send you copies under separate cover. Yesterday, Mr. Lion of Cathay Films let us use a car to drive around the island—all this and free movies. In other words, the red carpet treatment continues in our favor.

Chapter 24

Sudden Storm off Sumatra

The crew collected provisions for the next leg of their journey and said farewell to Blackie and his radio equipment. They set sail from Penang, beginning their crossing of first the Andaman Sea and then the Bay of Bengal en route to Colombo, Ceylon. On May 6, the first day out of Penang, Steve was on the helm at 0400 hours feeling a little cold in the late night breeze. He was rather tired from his experience in Penang. It was at the end of his three-hour watch and nearly time to wake Walt, who was scheduled next on shift. A ship was off ahead in the distance and Steve was able to see its red navigation light, meaning it was crossing their path heading south. There was no danger of collision.

Suddenly, however, a slight gust of wind came from behind. Steve countered with a move to port to keep the boat from jibing (a situation in which the mainsail and the jib are caught by the wind and slammed from one side to the other across the boat, which can easily do serious damage to the rigging and injure anyone in its path). The next thing Steve knew, the boat was making a hard turn into the wind and white water was coming into the cockpit. In barely a minute, the boat, under full sail, was running before a fifty to sixty-knot gale. "Emergency!" Steve yelled. "Everyone up. Take down the jib. Lower the main!"

Paul yelled from below that he had been thrown out of his bunk to the floor. Walt stuck his head out of the hatch, having difficulty keeping his balance. Steve yelled to Walt to let the sail out. By this time, rain was pouring down, drenching everything in the cockpit. Lightning flashed all about. Gou was terrified, crouching as close as he could to the steering pedestal and getting in the way.

For the first several moments it looked as though the *Suzy Wong* would lose her mast. The helm was nearly impossible to control and Gou wasn't making matters any easier inasmuch as the spokes from the helm struck him every time

Steve spun the wheel to keep the boat from pitching sideways. If Steve couldn't get the boat under control, they could capsize.

Steve shouted for Walt to take the helm so that he and the others could go forward to take down the sails. With difficulty, they managed to lower and secure the sails. J.D. was astride the Genoa jib, now down and flapping in the wind. The mainsail came down and it too was fluttering wildly in the wind. By now the crew was soaking wet, and all but Steve had been shocked out of a sound sleep. Gou ended up below deck, as Steve had picked him up by the scruff of the neck and backside and tossed him down below to get him out of the way of the wheel.

By 0500h the storm had subsided and the ship in the distance had mysteriously disappeared. The crew had just experienced what the coastal pilots call a "Sumatra," a fierce thunderstorm coming off the island of Sumatra to the south. These storms come up suddenly, without warning, and produce hurricane-force winds. They have caused many a craft to capsize, but luckily not the *Suzy Wong*. When the guys had time to reflect on the situation, they were immensely thankful that Walt, as silent and conservative as he was, had insisted that the stays and rigging be properly tested for strength back in Hong Kong.

Steve got little sleep in what remained of the night due to his wet clothes, a leaky hatch, and the wild motion of the sea. The others didn't fare so well either, but at least they had the benefit of a few hours of sleep before the night's Sumatra hit.

On the third day out, the crew ran into another squall line. This storm was less intense than the first one, but it still contributed to the most anxiety-ridden leg of the voyage thus far.

On May 10, after several days of fair sailing, the crew spotted Great Nicobar Island in the distance. Upon approaching the island, the Americans saw coming toward them a strange-looking dugout canoe with a number of native people aboard. The natives appeared to be as curious about the Americans as the Americans were about them. Coming within hailing distance, the natives suddenly turned about and headed away. Still, the

Americans had a chance to get a good look at their boat and at them. Their craft was sleek, with bow and stern coming to a very fine, decorative point. This was traditional ornamentation designed to keep the evil spirits away—a standard feature on all the local boats.

The Americans continued on towards Kondul Island in the Nicobars, where they planned to anchor and fill their water tanks before crossing the Bay of Bengal. A small boat with fully armed Indian soldiers then approached the *Suzy Wong*.

Nicobar militia in lateen-rigged canoe alongside *Suzy*, Andaman Sea

The crew had no idea what the problem was. The soldiers didn't speak English, and the Americans didn't speak any of the countless Indian dialects they might have needed to communicate with the soldiers. As the distance between the boats narrowed, the tensions began to rise and the Americans prepared for possible trouble by readying the ship's weapons, but keeping them out of sight to avoid an unwanted confrontation. Soon, both sides saw there was no cause for alarm, so the crew put their weapons away. Cooler heads prevailed and George invited the soldiers aboard the *Suzy Wong*.

Soldiers from Nicobar's Kondul Island welcomed aboard

George stood up, held out his hands to show he had no weapon, and motioned that he wanted permission to go down into the cabin to get something. When he returned, both his hands were out in front of him holding a bottle of Scotch. Everyone eagerly accepted a drink, and tensions eased. Steve suggested the soldiers might want to unload their guns. This was done, removing all apprehension from the situation. The soldiers then invited the crew to visit their island village.

Upon examining the soldiers' array of weapons, Steve determined that the soldiers couldn't have harmed the visiting sailors if they had tried. The bullets were all the wrong kind—their guns would have exploded in their own faces! The general assessment was that the soldiers were very inexperienced and, in all likelihood, had probably never encountered a sailboat like the *Suzy Wong*, or any hostile boat, for that matter.

It turned out that when the islanders saw the Chinese characters brilliantly emblazoned on *Suzy's* sail, they became suspicious that the Chinese had invaded their fishing waters. Once the *Suzy* crew explained that their boat was made in China and that the Chinese symbols merely spelled out the name of the boat, all went well.

After those two encounters, the Americans went ashore on Kondul Island in the Nicobar chain at the south end of the archipelago. They thought it was one of the most primitive places they had ever visited. To their horror and dismay, they could see that the children suffered from malnutrition and rickets, as evidenced by their grotesquely deformed hands and distended bellies.

Kondul Islanders at home; Nicobar Islands

The crew needed water for their long Bay of Bengal crossing. They located the village watering hole and saw that people, pigs, and chickens used it alike. The flies were thick and that reminded Paul of an old joke that he shared with the crew. "A guy goes into a diner and says, 'I'll have a piece of that raisin pie.' The waitress waves her hand over the pie, shooing the flies away, and says, 'It's custard!'"

It also reminded Steve that Commander Skidmore from Sangley Point, whose *Ping Po* sailing adventure had inspired this voyage, absolutely detested flies. He had a fly swatter on hand at all times and said that flies were the dirtiest things alive—"they either spit or shit every thirty seconds." Skidmore would not have approved of this watering hole, and after looking at the filthy water, the crew all agreed. They decided instead to ration their remaining water for the Bay of Bengal crossing, which would take about ten days.

They left the Nicobar Islands after just a few hours, the shortest stopover so far. They had no reason to stay any longer. There was no town. There was no water. It was time to go.

CHAPTER 25

MONSOON HITS WITH A VENGEANCE

The boat continued on its westward path across the Bay of Bengal, heading southwest toward Colombo, Ceylon. The crew was perfectly aware that they were in danger of running into the monsoon season at some point. They had been advised and warned, but their naiveté made them fearless, perhaps foolishly so.

The *Suzy Wong* had been six weeks late leaving Hong Kong. This meant they weren't going to make it across the Indian Ocean before the onset of the Southwest Monsoon, as originally planned. This weather phenomenon was expected to start around mid-May and continue for nearly six months. Sure enough, they were in the middle of the Bay of Bengal, four hundred miles from their next landfall, when the monsoon season commenced with a thunderstorm lasting twenty-four hours.

On May 14 the log recorded, "Stormy weather, heavy seas, and it is suspected we are getting the first of the SW Monsoon winds." The crew had a very uncomfortable night, as it was all hands on deck to ride out the storm. Steady, howling winds came from the southwest at forty to fifty miles per hour, blasting directly from where they were headed. They had no choice but to take down the large mainsail, which was too much sail to withstand that wind.

As the monsoon was beginning to alter their course and force them away from southern Ceylon, the crew decided to head northwest to Trincomalee on the northeast coast of Ceylon. This was the nearest port on a tack the crew could maintain during the storm with those conditions. They would have to worry about how to cross the Indian Ocean later.

For the next several days they sailed under black storm clouds, with only occasional clear patches of sky. It was nearly dark, even at midday. The high winds and heavy seas held relentlessly constant. Estimated Force 8 winds limited forward progress to almost nothing, as the crew had to rely only on the storm jib and mizzen sails.

The crew had no way of actually measuring wind speed so they used the Beaufort Wind Scale, which estimated wind speeds based on the effect of the wind upon the sea. For example, a Force 5 would have the wind at nineteen to twenty-four miles per hour. This would be considered a fresh breeze with moderate waves six to eight feet, many whitecaps, and some spray. A Force 8 sea would have winds at thirty-nine to forty-six miles per hour. This would be considered a gale with seas of eighteen to twenty-five feet and wave tops beginning to break into spray.

By May 20 there was still no letup in the wind. Contending with this much wind and high seas was simply exhausting. Somehow, the guys had to rest. They directed the boat into the wind in an attempt to "hove to" (an adjustment of the sails to hold the boat more or less in position). Unable to set the sails correctly, the crew suffered a seemingly endless night. The boat was at the mercy of the storm-driven sea.

During the middle of the night, they suffered yet another setback. The crew had taken down the #2, or working jib, to put up the storm jib. That night the #2 jib was washed overboard; it hadn't been tied down securely. This was a huge loss, as the sailors needed the #2 jib to balance the sails and propel the boat forward in a moderate to strong wind. The storm sail was just too small to do the job, and the Genoa jib was too large.

The inexperienced crew had no idea what they were going to do. They needed the driving force of a shortened, or reefed, mainsail to advance the boat in their northwest direction. Steve went to the cabin to get the sailing manual. For a laugh, he read to the crew that they should "reef the sail" (pull up and tie off) *before* leaving port and *before* high winds were expected. It was easy for the crew to see the humor in this instruction given their current situation. It may have been too late to reef the sail before the winds hit, but this idea was the only solution they had to work with now.

There were two rows of reef ties on the mainsail; one row of ties was about one-third of the way up the sail, and the second was two-thirds up. The idea was to reduce the sail area exposed to the wind. To do this, the crew had to first raise the sail all the way up, and then lower it to the appropriate row of ties, depending upon how much sail they wanted to leave exposed given the expected conditions. At each row of ties, they could secure that portion of the sail around the boom.

The crew was trying to get the job done despite the terrible conditions. Each time they raised the sail, the wind pushed the boat hard to one side, forcing it to come around into the wind. There was just too much wind to accomplish the task in this manner. They tried over and over, always with the same bad result. After twenty-four hours of effort, the crew still had not been able to reef the mainsail.

On the second day of struggling, they decided to use a different tactic. They turned the boat completely downwind, thereby reducing the relative force of the wind on the boat and the sail. They then attempted to raise the mainsail, being extra careful to keep the wind directly behind them. Any variation from this downwind direction resulted in the boat being knocked sideways and forced to come around into the wind. After a number of unsuccessful attempts, they were finally able to engage two sets of reef ties and resume their forward progress. In the midst of the mayhem, the crew had to chart a revised course. They had lost almost fifty miles since the onset of the monsoon!

Sailors use a variety of reference materials to navigate safely in specific ports. A comprehensive book published by the US Coast and Geodetic Survey (CGS) provides a detailed narrative description of sailing directions into most of the world's harbors along with descriptions of their entrance channels (to avoid obstacles). The crew had a port map for Colombo in their library, but they didn't have one for Trincomalee; their original sailing plan had not included this port.

They did, however, have a large area chart for this part of the Indian Ocean, and George was able to sketch a port map for Trincomalee by converting the book's written directions into a visual image on paper. By using George's makeshift map and sailing under a greatly reduced mainsail, the crew was able to steer the boat on toward their new destination.

Late in the evening on May 21, their estimated position put the boat fifty miles southeast of Trincomalee, and they finally spotted the Foul Point Lighthouse on the horizon. Log entries on May 22 noted that the boat had, "Passed abeam Foul Point…Passed abeam Round Island & entered the harbor, finding it a very pretty but windy spot…." George's improvised Trincomalee port map couldn't have been drawn more perfectly if he had actually been there in person.

They had survived the onset of the monsoon; a miracle considering they were woefully lacking in preparation for the situation. In retrospect, they learned that it might have been advisable to read up on emergency procedures *before* actually needing them.

Chapter 26

Safe Harbor

Trincomalee, Ceylon (now known as Sri Lanka) had a natural, deep-water harbor. It was large enough to accommodate the Royal Ceylon Navy, there to greet the *Suzy Wong* on May 22 when she arrived. Tying *Suzy* up to an assigned docking buoy proved to be a difficult task. The winds were strong and the engine lacked the muscle necessary to properly position the boat. With Walt at the helm, the crew tried a couple of times to maneuver the boat into position to catch the buoy. They reconfigured the sails and tried a third and fourth time, but each time they drew close, the wind blew the boat away. Their efforts became a source of amusement for members of the Ceylonese Navy, who were watching and laughing wildly. In the end, the navy sent out a small motorboat to help the crew tie *Suzy* up.

Finally in port and with *Suzy* safely secured, the crew was invited to eat with the Ceylonese Navy in their mess hall adjacent to the dock. They ate there only once, pretending to enjoy the meal while being traumatized by the spicy curry that burned the insides of their mouths. Their hosts swore that the cooks made the curry less spicy for the Americans, but that didn't seem to make a difference.

After the harrowing experience of the monsoon that nearly took their lives, the crew needed a break. Ceylon was a pretty nice place for passing the time, making repairs, waiting out the monsoon, and trying to figure out what to do next. It was also a good time to learn about this exotic country and appreciate what it had to offer.

Adorned with lush tropical forests, white sandy beaches, and diverse landscapes, its natural beauty made it quite apparent to the crew why Ceylon was often called, "The Pearl of the Indian Ocean." The country had one of the world's longest documented histories, attributed to the many different ethnic communities on the island: the Sinhalese majority in the south, the

Tamil minority in the north, and the Moors, Burghers, Kaffirs, Malays, and aboriginal Vedda people spread throughout. Ceylon had also been a center for the Buddhist religion and culture since ancient times and was one of the few remaining abodes of Buddhism in south Asia.

Located along the path of the major sea routes, this island-nation to the southeast of mainland India had long been a strategic naval link between west Asia and Southeast Asia. Ceylon became even more prized when traders discovered that it had abundant natural resources of tea, coffee, coconuts, rubber, and, most importantly, cinnamon, which is native to the country.

With such a long, important seafaring history, Ceylon was indeed the perfect place for the crew to rest, replenish, repair, and recoup. It was particularly nice for them when another small boat, the *Bellicose*, tied up close to theirs at the naval dock. A Japanese woman and her American husband owned the *Bellicose*. The husband would dive for fresh lobster every day and share his catch with the crew.

Suzy's sailors began their search for a sailmaker to provide a replacement for the #2 jib that was lost at sea. One would have thought that in such a seafaring land, sailmakers would be everywhere. But that wasn't the case. The local boats were used for fishing and transport, propelled mostly by sail power. Being wide and clunky, those boats were extremely stable for the kind of service they provided. Their sails were big, baggy pieces of canvas, not the kind used on an ocean racing craft such as the *Suzy Wong*.

Finding no legitimate sailmaker who could reproduce the jib, they decided that Omar, the tentmaker, would have to suffice for the job. The cloth he used to make the sail was the traditional soft, billowy canvas, and their replacement sail was immediately and affectionately dubbed the "rag." It wasn't pretty, but it would have to do.

A small hotel in town that served mostly Western cuisine became the crew's regular eating spot and watering hole. This hotel was also home to a number of Russian agricultural aid workers helping the Ceylonese government with their sugar cane crop. Knowing that both superpowers had spies in many countries, and experiencing the tension the world was under due to the Cold War, the crew just had to find out what the Russians were up to.

The *Suzy Wong* sailors had a casual way about them. They were always willing to chat with people they just met, and always out to have a good time. The Russians, on the other hand, were just plain stiff—almost rigid in their demeanor. They came down to eat at their assigned table with an aloofness and formality that was off-putting. They almost never said a word of greeting or even cracked a smile. George found this amusing and took it upon himself to go over and investigate the situation. When he came back, he was howling with laughter. Their project in the sugarcane fields had come to an abrupt halt because the Russians couldn't keep the elephants from stomping all over the crops. It seemed the elephants had a sweet tooth for the sugar cane and nothing could keep the huge beasts from satisfying that craving.

The Ceylon National Railway had some of the most magnificent scenic routes in the world. Dating back to the mid-nineteenth century, almost a thousand miles of track had been built by 1960 to transport harvested tea, coffee, and other goods across the island to Colombo.

One day Paul and Steve took a pleasurable train trip from Trincomalee across the island to the capital city, Colombo. This journey took them over rolling hills and past hundreds of waterfalls, alongside tropical tea plantations on Ceylon's high plateau, through the ancient capital of Kandy, and past the mountain resorts where the British colonials often went in summertime to escape Ceylon's oppressive heat.

The primary purpose of their train trip to Colombo was to pick up the shipmates' mail at the American Embassy. Mail was extremely important to the crew, and especially to Paul. He was eager to receive news from Mary and many others with whom he was corresponding. Mail for the crew was sent to the American diplomatic mission in the various ports, usually an embassy or consulate.

Once in Colombo, Paul and Steve looked for a cheap place to stay. The US Consulate directed them to an elderly widow, Mrs. Edmund Rodrigo, who, on occasion, rented out rooms to visiting foreigners. She was a devout Buddhist and a very interesting person. Her philosophy was, "If you own something, you become its slave, not its master!" She used the example of owning an automobile to illustrate her point: "You have to work to keep an automobile in good condition or it deteriorates; you have to work to buy fuel; and you have safety responsibilities." Her bottom-line question was, "Do you want to be the master or the slave?" Her logic was impeccable, but it was a personal philosophy that was completely foreign to Paul and Steve.

Paul had been exchanging letters with Mary since they parted in Hong Kong. However, there were frequent delays in the long-distance mail delivery system and sometimes the letters didn't arrive in proper sequence, or at all. The silence caused Paul some heart-rending angst. In a letter to her dated May 27, 1960, he wrote the following:

> My dearest Mary,
>
> I think we should start numbering our letters in case some are lost. I'll start this with #1. We are staying in a private home owned by an elderly woman. She is quite a person. Her husband was Secretary of Agriculture for Ceylon for many years. She has a huge home and rents a room out to tourists from time to time. She is well educated, speaks both English and Ceylonese, and has traveled all over the world. Two years ago seven women were invited to visit Red China as guests and she was one of them. Honestly, honey, this sounds trite, but we have learned so much just talking with her. I know you would enjoy this sort of thing.

Mary replied and labeled her letter number #1 as well:

> My dear Paul,
>
> Just received your letter #1 and was so glad to hear from you. I think it is probably a good idea to number the letters. The woman sounds wonderfully interesting. How I would love to be able to talk with her too! I am so glad to see that you find this sort of thing so interesting and stimulating, for you know how much I enjoy such. You should be able to learn much there in Ceylon, and I do hope you are taking notes or will remember the details so that you can tell me.

The next day, Paul and Steve began their train trip back over the mountains to Trincomalee Port. As it turned out, they almost missed the train. They had no tickets and were loaded down with two large boxes of canned fruits and vegetables. Steve found a porter and Paul hurriedly bought some tickets. Once on board, they couldn't find seats in any of the cars. And there were no sleeper berths available to them since they were traveling second class. Finally, a conductor said they could use a car marked "Ladies Only" on the condition that they move if any women asked to have their seats.

Paul and Steve settled into the ladies' car. They pulled down the blinds of their compartment, stretched out on the seats, and prepared to get a good, long sleep since the 180-mile trip would take up to ten hours. After just two hours, however, a noisy Ceylonese military officer boarded the train at a station stop. He came in slamming the door behind him and then opened the window to yell goodbye to someone on the platform. Paul woke up quite annoyed, but Steve, always a heavy sleeper, didn't stir.

The military man, speaking in a broken English accent, wanted to start up a conversation with Paul. But Paul just wanted to go back to sleep. When it finally became apparent that Paul didn't want to chat, the man woke Steve. He asked Steve to adjust his position so he could put his feet up. Four stops later, the man went out to get some tea and came back in a huff. He grabbed his luggage, stomped out, and slammed the door behind him, shouting, "It's a ruddy ladies' compartment!" Steve and Paul's good night's sleep had been ruined, but they had a hearty laugh at the chap and his indignation.

Press agent Irving Hoffman sent notes to the crew along the way. Some of them reached the crew promptly, and some didn't. He had written a special delivery letter that Paul and Steve picked up at the American Embassy in Colombo. But another letter he wrote didn't make it to Ceylon in time so it, along with some other mail, was forwarded to the crew's next port of call. Wherever they went, the crew's huge load of mail—sometimes thirty or forty pieces—made the locals wonder what kind of celebrities they had in their midst. Usually, that celebrity was just Paul, to whom most of the mail was addressed.

The monsoon continued to rage and the guys waited. Paul started growing a beard and his shipmates thought he was beginning to look like Fidel Castro. Steve decided to attempt the grizzled sailor look and stopped shaving as well. The crew was bored and they were in a quandary as to what to do next. They still hadn't figured out how they were going to cross the Indian Ocean.

Chapter 27

Drop and Hop

The guys knew that they couldn't sail across the Indian Ocean directly into the full force of the Southwest Monsoon. Their carefully considered options were as follows:

1. Stay in Ceylon until the monsoon was over in November.

2. Drop south of the equator to escape the monsoon, island hop to the Maldives and Seychelles islands, then travel north around the Horn of Africa (Cape Guardafui) and up the Red Sea to the Suez Canal.

3. Sail south all the way along the east coast of Africa, through the channel between Mozambique on the mainland and the island of Madagascar, around the Cape of Good Hope in South Africa, and then north across the Atlantic Ocean toward the United States.

4. Have the boat put on a ship and taken to the Mediterranean.

The options were hashed and rehashed. The *Suzy Wong* crew was crazed for adventure, so staying in Ceylon for another five months would be maddening. Sailing around the entire continent of Africa would take too long and wouldn't meet any of the trip's original objectives, which included sailing the Mediterranean in the summer and the Caribbean in the winter. And the idea of putting the *Suzy Wong* onto another ship was not only costly (and not as much fun), but it simply wasn't possible, as there were no ships available to transport them.

They decided that the only acceptable option was to drop and hop from Ceylon to the Maldive Islands, and then on to the Seychelles, proceeding from there back onto their original course. Truth be told, the guys were most looking forward to traveling the Mediterranean, where they imagined beautiful girls would greet them at every port.

After a prolonged stay of three weeks in Ceylon (from May 22 until June 12), they finally bid farewell to the Royal Ceylonese Navy and set sail. On June 12, 1960, the log stated, "Departed Trincomalee—Five normal crew members & one dog are aboard." They headed southeast through the troughs of the monsoon, bound for the Royal Air Force's staging post on Gan in the Maldive Islands. They had to contend with rough seas and strong southwesterly winds all day and night.

Soon after leaving Trincomalee, in the midst of rough seas, crew member J.D. Malone became ill. J.D. had signed on in Hong Kong as a paying passenger and joined the boat in Singapore. Now he was having difficulty urinating and was obviously in a great deal of pain, so Walt, Paul, Steve, and George all took turns trying to calm him. They tried pouring water over his private parts to provide some degree of comfort, but that did little good. As they proceeded south toward the equator, the rough seas subsided, and fortuitously so did J.D.'s anxiety. He was able to urinate, which provided some relief, but he was still not in good shape.

On June 16, 1960, the *Suzy Wong* crossed the equator into the more tranquil seas of the southern hemisphere. This was a momentous occasion—it was the first such crossing for crew and dog. They had a strict shipboard rule against alcohol consumption while at sea. But they made an exception this one time. They all had a drink to celebrate.

On June 19 things started to go bad. One of the crew let the jib halyard slip from his hands and it went flying to the top of the fifty-five-foot mast, jamming in the pulley. Without this halyard, the jib could not be raised.

Then, on June 20, Paul took to his bunk in the cabin with stomach trouble. This left them with yet another ill crew member. With no expertise and only medical manuals, they had to let nature take its course.

To make matters worse, they ended up with engine trouble. They first noticed there was a problem when they revved the engine and the boat didn't move forward. George, an expert swimmer, dove underneath the boat to see if he could spot the problem. He discovered that the engine shaft was turning, but the propeller was not. The propeller had somehow become freewheeling on the shaft.

He swam back to the surface to report the problem. They knew they were in a tough spot. There was nothing around them but hundreds of miles of open ocean in all directions—no wind, no motor, no radio to call for help, and no repair shop. The *Suzy Wong* was in the doldrums of the Indian Ocean, stuck in a calm area between the trade winds to the south and the monsoon to the north. The boat was becalmed without the use of its engine or its jib. Moreover, with just the main and mizzen, the boat was unbalanced as a sailing craft.

The first priority was to repair the propeller, if they could. The halyard would have to wait. George dove back into the water to retrieve the propeller and shaft. He lashed them together with a line and brought them to the surface. Using a cork from a wine bottle, the crew then plugged the shaft hole from the inside to prevent water from coming in. They examined both parts and saw that the shaft key was worn and could not engage the propeller. The log recorded, "Lost prop due to broken and mauled shaft key."

On the high seas, they had limited resources for making repairs. But George and Walt were clever and creative. They used the tin from a can of British sugar biscuits (labeled "Peek Freans") to shim the key slot between the propeller and the shaft so it would hold its connection. George then swam under the boat yet again and somehow managed to insert the propeller and shaft back in place, taking quick trips to the surface for gulps of air. The cookie-tin-fix worked well enough, but George knew it would need further repairs at their next port of call.

The boat limped along toward the Maldives with the propeller just barely working. The weather cooperated, with fair winds from the southeast pushing the *Suzy Wong* gently and slowly in the desired direction.

Of course, they still had the halyard problem to correct. The boat had two halyards going up the main mast, one for the mainsail and another for the jib or spinnaker. Each halyard was attached to the tip of a sail, going up through a pulley at the top of the mast and down the other side to the deck. In order to pull a sail up, they had to pull down on the halyard. At some point, someone neglected to fasten the sail properly, and the result was not good. The halyard had flown up to the top of the mast without the sail.

One of them would have to go aloft on the boson's chair to fetch the jammed halyard. They drew straws to see who would perform this dangerous task. Simply standing on the deck was tricky enough, but fifty-five feet above deck the rocking effect would be treacherous. Of all people, J.D. drew the short straw. Unfortunately, he was still quite sick and couldn't perform this task. Three days after Paul had taken ill, he was still in his bunk showing no sign of improvement either, despite the administration of mineral oil to settle his roiling stomach.

With Paul and J.D. both out of the running, the crew selected Steve. He was one of the more daring crew members and he was also a bit lighter than either George or Walt. Steve rode the boson's chair to the top of the mast, hanging on for dear life, and retrieved the halyard. Safely back on deck, he used the reacquired halyard to raise the Genoa jib. With the mizzen sail at the stern and the Genoa jib in the bow, the boat was once again balanced, enabling it to sail normally.

After ten more days of arduous sailing, they caught sight of the British Royal Air Force military airbase on Gan Island, commonly known as RAF Gan. The military base was on Addu Atoll, the southernmost island that was part of the larger Maldive island archipelago. The fact that the crew was able to locate this atoll in the middle of the Indian Ocean was proof of Walt's skill as a navigator. With the island's low profile, it was impossible to see it until they were practically upon it. It would have been very easy to miss. In a vast ocean, this was a tiny target, and Walt hit the bull's-eye.

Chapter 28

Specks in the Sea

After sailing below the equator and coming from the east to the Maldives archipelago, the *Suzy Wong* arrived at the capital city of Malé on June 30. The Republic of the Maldives looked no more imposing than a few specks in the sea; it was the lowest country on the planet, with its highest point no more than eight feet above sea level. The crew tied up at a buoy and then jumped through the appropriate bureaucratic hoops to register their arrival in the country with the port director and security. On July 2 the *Suzy Wong* moved to the pier at the Royal Air Force Gan military base to perform maintenance and repairs.

This boat, suddenly having appeared from nowhere on their shore, made the Brits justifiably more than a little curious. The RAF officers were, at first, suspicious that the Americans were CIA types, or even Russian spies. After all, 1960 was in an era of Cold War tensions. The Chinese were in the middle of their Great Leap Forward, and just the previous month American pilot Gary Powers had been shot down while on a reconnaissance mission over Russia, much to the embarrassment of President Dwight D. Eisenhower. During the *Suzy Wong's* passage from Ceylon to the Maldives, the crew had picked up shortwave radio broadcasts from the *Voice of America*, the *BBC*, *Peiping Polly in China*, and the *Voice of Moscow*—each with its own version of the Gary Powers incident. The crew thought war might break out at any moment.

When the British questioned George, he didn't realize how serious they were. He was his jovial self, not thinking about the rest of the world heading for turmoil. Jokingly playing the spy, he responded to their wariness, "Not to worry, we finished all our sonar gradients last night." The officer he was talking to went ballistic. Being flippant about espionage was not amusing, and it took hours of explanation to calm the officer down. In fact, the British even contacted the naval station at Sangley Point in the Philippines to check out the crew's story.

Once the misunderstanding had been resolved, the Brits greeted the Americans with a more hearty welcome. The members of the officers' club invited the crew to join them for food, drink, and some entertainment. For the Brits, being on Gan for a long tour of duty was a bit like being confined to prison. They were surrounded by water, and the island provided little in the way of topographical variety. The arrival of the *Suzy Wong* was the biggest distraction the Brits had had in nearly a year. They were eager to hear the tales of the world-traveling celebrities.

On July 4 Paul wrote to Mary:

> The island here is small, about two miles long and three-fourths of a mile wide. There is an airstrip running the full length of the small landmass extending out in either direction into the lagoon. There are buildings for the five hundred RAF military personnel that live here year round. Aside from that, there is nothing. The water is pretty—from very light blue to a deep jade green, and those colors change with different water depths and light conditions. It's a tough grind for these Brits to spend a year here, but it's a beautiful place to spend a week or two.

The Americans found there was always something to do at night on the island of Gan—like carousing, telling jokes, and raising all kinds of hell in every mess hall where they were invited. The next two weeks passed quite pleasantly.

One night at a club, however, a British officer became rowdy and loud about his opinion of Americans. It was the Fourth of July and, needless to say, the British didn't celebrate this most American of holidays. This officer got himself quite riled up and boasted with his insufferably British stiff upper lip and air of superiority, "We should have marched over and kicked your 'arses' at the end of the war!" Walt, who was a man of few words, took a deep breath and drawled in his best Tennessee accent, "A-g-a-i-n?" He reminded the drunken officer that, in fact, the Brits had not done such a good job of besting the Americans during the Revolutionary War.

Redirecting their attention to the damaged propeller and shaft, the crew asked if the Brits had any ideas about what could be done. The Americans described how they had shimmed the propeller shaft mid-ocean. The Brits offered to put *Suzy* in dry dock and examine her carefully, at which point they quickly saw what needed to be done. The Brits put one of their own military boats (similar to an American PT boat) out of commission so they could remove its shaft and install it into *Suzy*. The metal for this shaft was really strong and corrosion resistant—only the best for the Royal Air Force—which translated into an upgrade for the *Suzy Wong*. They machined the shaft to fit and reinstalled the propeller. All this came at no charge to the Americans.

Even after this show of generosity, the Brits asked if there was anything else they could do to help. Not missing a beat, Paul said, half in jest, "Well, yes, we could use some help getting our mail from the American Consulate in Aden." Unbeknownst to the crew, the British had already sent a fighter jet to Yemen to collect the crew's mail. When they saw the stack of cards and letters, the crew was amazed at how far the Brits had gone to accommodate them.

Still, there was one more request; it was a personal one from Paul. He asked if he could pay to send a telegram to his girlfriend, Mary, now stationed at the American Embassy in Madrid. The Brits assured Paul that it would be no problem, so Paul wrote a mushy telegram and off it went, again at no charge. The kicker was that, because it was sent from an RAF base to an American Embassy, it was automatically coded as "Top Secret." This meant that when the telegram arrived in Madrid at 4:00 a.m., the marines were called out of bed to decode it immediately. When Mary got to her desk the next morning, she was greeted by a gathering of amused marines holding a decoded, romantic message. She would be ribbed about her "Top Secret" telegram for months to come.

During their Maldives revels, the Americans met a physician who was a rugby player, formerly with the British National Team. Paul had also tried his hand at rugby on occasion and he struck up a friendly conversation with the man. Friendly banter soon turned into a macho competition to see who could bash his head through the wall of the room. It wasn't supposed to hurt too much, as long as they missed the structural wall joist—which was not always the case. With brains rattled, no one was really sure who, if anyone, was the winner.

One day, an Indian man pulled alongside the docked *Suzy* in his small boat. He indicated that he wanted to come aboard and look around. Gou stood perfectly still at the gangway and stared relentlessly at this stranger. The man looked apprehensively at Gou and back at the crew. Not knowing the man's intentions, Paul warned him that the dog had killed someone who had trespassed, so it was too dangerous for him to come aboard. The man remained in his boat, but he wanted to know how much the *Suzy Wong* was worth. The crew told him $25,000. He nodded and paddled away.

The next day, the man came back with a large lady's handbag. He said he wanted to buy the boat. He opened the lady's purse to reveal piles of British pounds and American dollars. Paul felt sure there had to be more than $25,000 inside! It turned out he was a trader and he probably would have sold his own mother for the right price. Paul made it clear to the man that they still needed the boat to finish their voyage and that *Suzy* was not for sale.

As the unofficial publicity liaison for the crew, Paul met the president of the People's Council of Addu Atoll, Mr. A. Afif Didi, who asked if there was any special favor he could do for the crew. Paul told Mr. Didi that he had a beautiful girlfriend in Madrid who would appreciate receiving some of the Maldives' wonderful seashells. Didi asked to see Mary's picture, and then he agreed to mail the shells right away.

Mr. Didi believed, for some inexplicable reason, that the *Suzy Wong* was somehow an official envoy of the president of the United States. He expected that the crew would forward the country's best wishes to President Eisenhower. The man might have assumed that the president of the United States would personally know each of his "subjects" just as Mr. Didi did on Addu Atoll.

At this port of call the crew said goodbye to crew member-passenger J.D. Malone, who decided not to continue the trip due to medical concerns. The British doctor at Gan diagnosed his condition as uremic poisoning, due most likely to the stress of being at sea. The doctor said that it very well might occur again, so J.D. thought it best to return home, hopping on an RAF flight to London before continuing on to the States. Crossing from Ceylon through the monsoon to get to the Maldives had been traumatic for him, and not exactly the relaxing vacation he had in mind.

On the morning of July 11, *Suzy*'s sailors prepared the boat to depart the Maldives, and many of the RAF officers' personnel came to the pier to see them off. While they were loading the boat, the sky suddenly turned black, and a cloudburst dumped nearly two inches of rain on them in what seemed an instant. The crew hadn't managed to get their gear aboard before the rain hit and they were thoroughly soaked by the shower, which then dissipated as quickly as it had formed.

Walt, George, and Steve leaving Maldives—Next stop, Seychelles Islands

The *Suzy Wong* cast off and cleared the lagoon, heading for the Seychelles with just the four original crew members and Gou on board. In keeping with the rebellious behavior they had exhibited while at Gan, the crew had stolen the base commander's insignia flag from his car. They had run it up *Suzy*'s mast and pointed to it as they sailed away. After about thirty minutes an RAF air-sea rescue boat approached *Suzy* at a high rate of speed. Paul said, "After all the hell we raised, can't they take a joke?" When the craft came barreling alongside *Suzy*, the crew was ready to surrender the flag, but that wasn't what the Brits wanted. George had bought some fine English cheese before their departure and had left it in one of the Brits' refrigerators. "You forgot your cheese!" they shouted, and tossed the package toward the *Suzy Wong*. But the throw was short and the cheese went into the water, where it promptly sank. So in the end, the crew got the flag…and the fish got the cheese!

Surprise! Royal Air Force crash boat chases *Suzy*, Indian Ocean

The crew had also bought scotch whiskey from the commissary on Gan. The price was so ridiculously low, with no taxes, that they bought a small supply. Fortunately, they remembered to stow the scotch on board the boat before pulling up the anchor, or else that stock might have wound up in the ocean along with the cheese.

Several days earlier, RAF Gan's commander had asked the Americans to participate in an air-sea rescue exercise while *Suzy* was en route to the Seychelles. The crew had agreed, so the Brits gave them a homing device which was to be turned on at a precise time each day. When the base received the signal from *Suzy* simulating a vessel in distress, the RAF would practice their air-sea rescue.

The first two days, right on schedule, the crew turned on the homing device and an RAF airplane appeared overhead, circled, dipped its wings, and flew away. On the third day, though, the plane didn't appear. The Americans thought there must have been a malfunction in the signal equipment. There was no way they could have known that the RAF was busy performing a real air-sea rescue operation that day.

CHAPTER 29

"SHOOTING" THE STARS

While still preparing for their voyage back in Hong Kong, the crew had scrounged up nautical charts, a current nautical almanac, and a couple of old sextants either from the US Navy or Hong Kong's ship junkyards. After their rushed departure and upon close examination of the boat's provisions, they discovered that the spherical trigonometry reduction table had been left behind, making it impossible to execute the necessary calculations when they had to establish their position by celestial means.

Being highly trained by the US Navy in celestial procedures for both surface and airborne navigation, Walt was the one who was designated to find their way across the oceans on the *Suzy Wong*. However, the first leg of the voyage from Hong Kong to Manila revealed to Walt that he had more to learn regarding navigation. While Walt was in Manila fulfilling his Naval Reserve active duty training, he made it a point to focus on becoming more familiar with using a sextant and reading the nautical tables used for calculating a vessel's position at sea. This was crucial for their voyage.

Because of its accuracy in measuring angles, the sextant has been used for over two hundred and fifty years to plot safe passage on the ocean. The designated navigator, using a sextant, must understand complex math to find his position on the globe. Spherical geometry is the language of the navigator, revolving around the concept that a circle has 360 degrees inside its circumference. A degree is divided into sixty minutes, and a minute is divided into sixty seconds.

To identify their position on the chart, the navigator would have to identify certain stars and then take a measurement of the angle between the star and the horizon at an exact point in time. The boat's shortwave radio could pick up international time ticks twice each hour. The crew used these time markers to set the boat's clock, which served as its chronometer. If the crew missed by only a second, the true location could be off by as much as ten miles. Shooting a star would result in a line drawn perpendicular to the direction of that star on a chart. The crew would repeat this several times, resulting in a triangle, sometimes referred to a "cocked hat" or a "fix."

To shoot the stars with a sextant aboard a sailboat meant standing on the deck and hanging on to the rigging while being tossed back and forth by the waves. A second person would note the exact time the angle was taken. Dusk can last for an hour up north, but closer to the equator there is a window of only about fifteen minutes when one can see both the star and the horizon. As a result, one must work fast. Once they had shot four or five stars and recorded the angles, it generally took the navigator about two hours to work out their position.

George takes noon sighting for latitude, Indian Ocean

Every now and then, the crew would take a noontime shot of the sun to determine their latitude, figuring out how far north or south they were. They had to use a special filter on the sextant to protect their eyes from the intensity of the direct sunlight. On cloudy days or nights, they couldn't get a star fix for obvious reasons. This was when they had to use "dead reckoning" to estimate the duration, speed, and direction they were traveling, and then lay down their course line accordingly. When they were able to take the next star fix, the navigator would correct their position on the chart.

Three months earlier, both caution and navigational experience had saved them as they approached Singapore. They had been off course by more than a hundred miles and they would have hit a reef had they proceeded without obtaining a navigational reading. It's one thing to know how to sail, but if you don't know where you are, you can end up on the rocks, or just become lost at sea. With a sextant and a good chronometer providing the exact time, a professional navigator can measure a boat's position to within two miles. Walter got to the point where he could chart the *Suzy Wong's* position to within five miles—close enough to avoid trouble during the voyage.

Walt enjoys lunch while plotting *Suzy's* position, Indian Ocean

CHAPTER 30

A REMOTE PARADISE

There is no such thing as constant conditions on the open ocean. Weather systems coalesce around various landmasses and then go spiraling off over the water to connect or collide with other systems. A boat sailing on the ocean finds the weather changing at a moment's notice. *Suzy* had been heading southwest toward the Seychelles off the east coast of Tanzania in Africa. But by 0230h on July 14, she found herself deep within a squall line with rain and high winds pushing her away from her intended course toward the northwest. By the next afternoon, winds shifted back to the south, allowing for smooth sailing again.

When it was a crew member's shift at the helm (often three hours at a stretch, all by himself), he had ample time to think about many things. At night, without streetlights or light pollution of any kind, the sky was an amazing sight to behold. He could imagine the immense size of the heavens with billions of stars, like grains of sand on a beach. At midday, in the bright light, he might contemplate how his life had led him to be there at that very moment. And thoughts might certainly drift on to the possible dangers ahead.

Five months into the journey, the crew had grown confident in their ability to handle the boat. The *Suzy Wong* was solidly built and had stood up well through a number of rough sea conditions, so they weren't worried about their vessel's seaworthiness. The frightening thing was contemplating disaster—having to abandon ship if the worst possible scenario came to pass. Could they get the small dinghy and life raft untied from the cabin roof in time? Would the life raft hold air? These were the dark thoughts that often invaded the sailors' private moments. It would be foolish to ignore them entirely, but it also wouldn't do to linger too long upon potentially awful outcomes. Each man had to decide in his own way to concentrate on happier thoughts, lest the negative ones drive him crazy with worry.

On July 16 the water outlet tube from the engine broke at the muffler connection. With clear skies, smooth seas, and a strong southeasterly breeze, the crew had good sailing conditions, allowing them to shut off the engine and make needed repairs to the cooling system. On the following day, July 17, the boat was still headed southwest when they ran into more scattered squall activity with winds increasing to fifteen knots by nightfall. The boat had steady south-southeast winds into the morning of July 18, making for easier sailing. Given the robust winds they had encountered, the crew wasn't too surprised to learn that they had covered 150 nautical miles in just twenty-four hours. On the afternoon of July 20, they dropped anchor in Victoria Harbor, Mahe Island, part of the Seychelles group.

The Seychelles is an archipelago of 115 islands in the Indian Ocean, lying some thousand miles east of Tanzania and an equal distance northeast of the island of Madagascar. Most of the islands are uninhabited. Encountering them for the first time, early Dutch and Portuguese explorers believed they had discovered the uppermost mountaintops of the fabled lost continent of Atlantis. Reinforcing this belief was the fact that they found no mammalian life of any kind. They could only find turtles and birds living on the islands.

The Seychelles became notable in the nineteenth century as the repository for rescued African slaves. Whenever an international naval ship (whose country was opposed to slavery) intercepted slave ships bound for North America or Europe, the problem arose of what to do with the slaves. They had to be taken somewhere. They certainly couldn't be returned to their African homeland, as they would be killed or sold back into slavery. By mid-1850, hundreds of slave ships were coming from the island of Zanzibar and depositing former slaves on the shores of the Seychelles, where they could begin their "free" lives.

In 1960 the Seychelles had no airport because of the steep volcanic incline of the islands. The only transportation in and out of the Seychelles was by freighter. But, according to international law, freighters were only allowed twelve passengers, unless a medical doctor was on board. Approximately twelve freighters arrived each year. If someone wanted to visit, he would have to stay for at least a month until the next freighter came to take him back out again. Needless to say, tourists were infrequent.

The crew of the *Suzy Wong* knew nothing of these islands' history; their interests were inclined more toward aesthetic pleasures. Once they learned the basics—that the islands had been colonized by the French and then given to the British during the Treaty of Versailles after World War I—they understood that the Seychelles now had the best of both realms: fine French cooking and firm British law, all against a backdrop of beautiful scenery.

Suzy parked alongside Norwegian-built *Aren;* Victoria Harbor, Seychelles

Two days after their arrival, the Americans sailed around Mahe Island and dropped anchor off Beau Vallon Beach. The only small hotel charged $4.50 per person per night, which included the cost of a room, breakfast, lunch, dinner, and tea. The hotel was on the lee side of the island, meaning the beautiful beach had calm waters. Generous hosts frequently entertained the crew, who reciprocated by taking their hosts out for a sail with cocktails served on board.

On July 24 the *Suzy Wong* set off from Beau Vallon Beach with ten hotel guests for a day's sail to nearby Silhouette Island. By early afternoon, the boat had nearly reached its destination when the winds kicked up the waves and several passengers became seasick. The trip was curtailed and the boat sailed back to the lovely beach at Beau Vallon. Back on dry land, the guests wobbled off the boat, their stomachs still churning from the experience.

Beau Vallon was such a welcome change of pace that the Americans decided to stay there another five days. They had problems, however, making the anchor hold in the sandy bottom. The tide would rise and fall, lowering the boat onto the sand.

The first time this happened, it was late in the afternoon and Steve was the only crew member aboard. He was unable to pull the anchor up by driving the boat forward since the water was too shallow and the bottom of the boat was already touching the sand. His solution was to toss the anchor line overboard and back the boat into deeper water. Without an anchor, he had to hold the boat in this position using the engine until the rest of the crew spotted the boat, now much farther out from land than expected.

George, Paul, and Walt were not happy to learn that Steve had tossed the anchor line overboard, causing a lot of unnecessary work. They felt he could have just let the boat rest on the sandy bottom waiting for the tide to change. The three land-bound sailors had no choice but to swim to the boat. Together they had to jury-rig an auxiliary anchor to hold the boat in place until the next morning, when they could retrieve the regular anchor.

Steve's masthead view, leaving Seychelles Islands

On July 29 at 1300h the *Suzy Wong* departed Beau Vallon Beach and sailed back to Victoria Harbor, arriving there at the same time as a visiting British frigate. As usual, the Americans befriended the Brits. The frigate was on its way to Aden, and since the Americans would have to sail much the same course, they asked the Brits to send them a report informing them of weather and sea conditions around Cape Guardafui, Somalia.

Meanwhile, Paul decided it would be sporting fun and good exercise to play cricket for the local Wanderers team against the opposing Eaglets. The newspaper write-up of the game reported, "Eaglets registered their second defeat of the Wanderers, Sunday last…. Cardoza, our visiting American who was playing his first game of cricket ever, forgot everything when he got to the wicket and let the first ball through…." Paul's excuse was that the ball was a "bad one," a ball thrown below the knees. That would have meant something in American baseball, but, unfortunately, foul pitches had nothing to do with cricket.

Paul wrote Mary a letter dated July 25 stating:

> At the moment I ache in every muscle, sinew, joint, limb, and bone. Between soccer on Saturday, cricket on Sunday, and rugby this afternoon, I feel like I've been through the mill. I guess I'm a bit out of shape due to the lack of exercise aboard *Suzy*.

The weather had been poor, with rain squalls every day. Paul and Steve had planned to climb a nearby hill before the rugby game, but it was too wet. The rain and overcast sky kept the crew from many of their preferred activities, including getting good photographs. The locals said the weather was unusual, but the islands were south of the equator and it was right in the middle of their winter.

Tamoogee's was the name of a large general store in Victoria run by East Indians. Paul stopped in and became acquainted with the owner and some of the customers. He played chess at Tamoogee's almost every day, polishing his rusty skills. As he did with all card games and matches of strategy, Paul played chess exceedingly well.

Sharkie Clark was an old Brit and the proprietor of a small guesthouse next to Victoria Harbor. Years earlier, London doctors told him that he had only one year to live. He had visited the Seychelles during the war and had promised himself he'd go back so he could die in paradise. After his diagnosis, he picked up and moved to the Seychelles.

Sharkie was a bit of a paradox. He had a soft heart and a weird sense of humor. He hired people with handicaps, or those who were misfits in society, helping them generously, but then he'd give them unflattering names. One young man was not all there mentally, so Sharkie called him Dummy, while another man with physical difficulties got named Tipsy.

Sharkie took in a woman who was a social outcast because she had had a daughter out of wedlock. This unwed mother was smart and hardworking and she ran Sharkie's hotel business. The crew could never remember the woman's name, but they wouldn't forget her daughter, Sheila, who was also smart and had received schooling in London for two years. Sheila was drop-dead gorgeous and she liked to prance around in a bikini. Paul said hers was the first bikini he had ever seen. All four of the guys found her to be highly desirable, but her protective mother made it very clear that no funny business was allowed.

Paul was resourceful and his mind worked quickly whenever there were ladies around. He decided that now would be a good time to catch up on his correspondence. Since Sheila worked for the Seychelles government as a secretary, she agreed to type letters that Paul would dictate to her. Each one of Paul's many pen pals got a personalized letter from him, typed perfectly by Sheila. In one particular letter, Paul mentioned that he had "lost twenty pounds" while aboard the *Suzy*. Sheila thought Paul had meant money so she typed the symbol for British pound sterling.

Written correspondence during the trip was a big deal with Paul. He invested a lot of time and money communicating his activities from afar, even if it was sometimes just a quick hello. He loved kids and had a lot of nieces and nephews, and they had begged him to send them postcards. In each exotic port he would remember the request and send out postcards to the kids. The list grew and grew until postage turned into one of his biggest expenses during the trip. He bought the most colorful and interesting stamps to add extra spice. He believed his correspondence made a lasting impression on these young people. It probably meant as much, if not more, to Paul.

The Arab men in Victoria wore interesting garments called "foutas," which looked like ladies' skirts to the Americans. They were cool in the hot weather and comfortable wear for the Seychelles. Wanting to fit in wherever they landed, all four guys tried wearing them. The experience of wrapping the fabric around their bodies made for a good laugh, but only Paul had any interest or developed any skill in donning a fouta. George and Walt thought the garments looked "girly" and used their inability to wrap the foutas properly as an excuse not to wear them.

As they were about to depart, the Americans received the weather report the Brits on the frigate had promised to send. It did not contain good news: Cape Guardafui, the peninsula off Somalia that juts into the opening of the Gulf of Aden (also known as the Horn of Africa), was experiencing high winds, rough seas, and poor visibility at this time of year. In spite of this lousy weather report, the crew cast off on August 2, 1960, with the usual fanfare from the many friends and acquaintances they had made during their short stay. Loaded down with gifts of bananas, breadfruit, and coconuts, they thanked everyone profusely. Once they had sailed out of sight, some of this booty got tossed overboard. The crew wasn't accustomed to a lot of the native food. Breadfruit was difficult to open and eat, and it was not very tasty. And too much coconut caused diarrhea. But they held on to the green bananas, as they would ripen over time.

CHAPTER 31

ONWARD TO AFRICA

At 1215h on August 2 the *Suzy Wong* crew cast off from Victoria bound for Aden, Yemen, a British protectorate located on the southwest tip of the Arabian Peninsula. Passing abeam of North Island, the boat soon hit heavy swells with southeasterly winds. The crew knew they were in for some rough sailing ahead. While they had already experienced some rather scary weather conditions, they had been extremely lucky for the most part. Now they were about to experience conditions that would tax their sailing abilities and their navigational skills to the utmost.

With poor visibility, Walter was going to have to rely on his dead reckoning skills, as they might not be able to see the stars to obtain a proper navigational fix. The ocean current was running north along the African coast in a narrow band and would give them a boost as far as speed was concerned, but that would be difficult to measure if all they could see was ocean.

What went through their minds was that they had never practiced a "man overboard" drill, something that is certainly recommended for any sailing craft in the open ocean. They decided to stage one soon after departing the Seychelles.

First, they had to figure out how they would maneuver the boat to "come about" (proceed in a changed direction) so the boat would pass back over the point where the man who had fallen overboard could be retrieved. They didn't want to practice the drill with an actual crew member, so they threw an old flotation cushion over the side instead. At that point, the seas were moderate with the wind quartering off the port side. Basically, they were heading downwind with the sails set wide to the starboard side. The carefully planned procedure seemed to be working well, bringing the boat back around to where the cushion should have been. They looked out at the water, and then back at each other with amazement. The cushion had disappeared! Was it possible they could actually lose a crewmate in the same way so quickly?

They hadn't anticipated that a lost sailor could be close, but still hidden by the rising and falling waves. Even from the highest point on deck, they never did spot the cushion. It was not an encouraging result. This episode caused a certain amount of anxiety amongst the crew. They silently made a mental note to be extra careful on deck and, of course, never to fall overboard.

As they traveled north, winds from the southwest picked up and the waves became correspondingly higher. Pretty soon the *Suzy Wong* was careening down the face of large waves, where she picked up speed and had a tendency to fishtail. The man at the helm had to counteract this effect by spinning the wheel in the opposite direction. Then he had to quickly reverse the direction of his spin to get ready for the next wave. There was no letup. As the seas grew worse, the helmsman had to expend increasingly more energy to keep the boat safely on course.

Not only did the helmsman have to be concerned about broaching (a sudden sideways shift that could damage or possibly capsize the boat), but also about jibing. One could easily be caught off guard for a moment and find the wind hitting the sail from the opposite side, violently swinging the boom across the boat and possibly taking out a crew member or some rigging in the process. Since this had happened several times in calmer waters and jarred everyone by its suddenness, the crew became even more alert given the severity of the weather conditions.

They knew ahead of time that they would be pressed to solve real problems along the way. The thinking shared by all was that such problems could be handled in a logical sequence. But here they were, finding it increasingly difficult with each passing moment to hold their intended course. Soon darkness would be upon them, and trying to maintain this strenuous steering procedure could very well lead to disaster. An answer had to be found quickly. They were faced with both a steering problem and safety concerns, as doubling back in such seas would be nearly impossible. They needed to rethink their safety and rescue procedures.

The first problem to solve was how to add drag to the boat when it was going down the face of a wave. George came up with the idea of trailing the hundred-foot anchor rope with knots tied approximately every five feet behind the boat whenever this wind and wave situation occurred. This solved, to some degree, the potential problem of a broach. Unexpectedly, it also improved their safety concern. If a crew member were to fall overboard, he could swim to the anchor line and catch hold. This way he would still be connected to the boat, dragging along behind it. Then, as soon as those on deck could respond, they'd pull him in.

It was painful to imagine, however, the awful fate that Gou would face if he were to fall overboard. In all likelihood, the dog wouldn't know to swim toward the trailing anchor line and bite it. The crew didn't like to confine Gou to the cabin, even during storms, so they hoped the dog would never fall overboard.

While still in the Seychelles, the men of the British frigate had given the Americans advice on how to navigate the treacherous waters along the Somali coast and how to round the eastern Horn of Africa, Cape Guardafui. The Brits told them that many ships, not knowing when to round the Cape, would turn too soon and crash into the cliffs. Other ships would turn too late and be driven farther out into the Gulf of Aden, where the winds pick up to near-hurricane force.

Such misjudgments were made when the navigator failed to take into account the five or six-knot northerly current running along the African coast. The Brits instructed the Americans to take the temperature of the water from time to time. At the point where the temperature dropped about ten degrees, they were told to start adding five to six knots to their speed calculations. The Brits also warned the Americans that the navigational light on top of the Cape sometimes didn't work or couldn't be seen. Dust from the African continent often obscured the cliff and the navigational light.

For a week the crew had steady southwest winds. Approaching the coast of Africa, the water temperature dropped suddenly. This was the awaited signal that they were now in the strong north-running current along the coast, running all the way up from the Cape of Good Hope at the southernmost tip of Africa. Sure enough, dust and sand from windstorms in Somalia, plus the combination of warm and cold waters mixing, decreased visibility greatly.

The *Suzy Wong* made fast time, sailing with gale force winds and strong currents propelling them forward through rough seas. Each crew member had to work harder than ever during his watch to keep the boat on course and free from broaching or jibing. At the helm, the steering wheel's eight handles made it easy to grab. But with gale force winds, these handles could slip out of their hands and catch them in the ribs or the legs. Having to use their entire bodies to hold the wheel steady, they became weary with sore arms and bruised legs. Because of the strenuous work and extra concentration needed at the helm, shift times were shortened.

On August 5 they hit squalls in the early morning with winds gusting to thirty knots. By August 8 winds and seas increased even more as they neared Cape Guardafui. They knew if they didn't stay on course and spot the Cape, they would be blown into the Gulf of Aden, where the wind would increase substantially. This prospect bothered the crew, particularly if visibility remained poor as they approached the Cape at dusk. Walter had been able to navigate to RAF Gan with precision, but in this instance, the added current was the wild card.

The dreaded "Horn of Africa;" Cape Guardafui, Somalia

On August 9 they sighted Cape Guardafui just at sundown, with the huge cliffs rising four hundred feet straight up from the sea. The dust in the air made the Cape look more distant than it actually was, so it was just luck that they arrived at this time of day when they could easily see this treacherous navigational hazard. Walter had effectively gained credibility as their navigator. He had made the navigational adjustments correctly and they rounded the Horn of Africa successfully, never coming dangerously close to the cliffs. Then, quite suddenly, the rough seas and wind died almost completely, as if the crew had never had to contend with them at all. The water temperature rose dramatically by twenty degrees. At long last, after many weeks of sailing, the *Suzy Wong* was free of the Southwest Indian Ocean Monsoon.

After their exhausting sail, the crew needed a break. On August 10 they dropped anchor off a small beach on the Somali coast. All four men and Gou decided to swim ashore for some much-needed time off the boat.

In all their travels thus far, Paul had never taken the opportunity to swim more than a few dozen yards. With Gou not too far away showing him how it was done, Paul demonstrated that he had learned to dog paddle. He swam, unaided, the distance of about a hundred yards from boat to shore.

Following World War II, Britain retained control of the northern stretches of Somaliland along the Gulf of Aden, calling it British Somaliland. In November 1949, the United Nations granted Italy trusteeship of the eastern stretches of the country along the Indian Ocean, known as Italian Somaliland. On June 26, 1960, the northern territory gained its independence, with the eastern province following suit five days later. On July 1, 1960, the two territories united to form the Somali Republic—more commonly known as Somalia. With the two territories combining, Somalia now had the longest coastline of the entire continent of Africa, measuring 1,880 miles.

The four sailors didn't know they had just landed in the world's newest country; what they saw was an arid, rocky coast that didn't impress them much. They were on an isolated stretch of beach along the northern coast of Somalia, far from any towns or people. The Americans had landed on the Guban, where the terrain was flat and barren with no vegetation as far as the eye could see. The sandblasted landscape had sharp lava rocks that cut the pads of Gou's delicate pink paws. The crew didn't stay onshore for long.

Steve and Gou explore desolate beach; Northern Somalia

That afternoon, resuming their course for Aden, they saw a large dark cloud swirling toward them. But it didn't move like a normal storm cloud. As it came closer, they realized it was a swarm of locusts. The strong winds off the African mainland were blowing these insects out to sea. Many seemed to be heading for the white sails of the boat, perhaps to catch it as it sailed along. Most missed the mark and landed in the sea. Some were lucky, at least for a short while, and clung to the sails. Gou now had something to do to occupy his time. He ran around the deck pouncing and snapping at the locusts. All hands sprang into action and shook the sails and rigging to dislodge them. It didn't take long before all the insects had either flown off or been swept away by the breeze that brought them.

Being hit by a swarm of locusts was a most unexpected experience for the crew of the *Suzy Wong*. They were anxious to rid their boat of them to protect the sails. Locusts start off as harmless little light green grasshoppers until the rains come and they change to a dusty camouflage tan. At that point, they congregate into voracious swarms so large and dangerous they can block out the sun and swirl into a munching plague that strikes fear into the hearts of peasant farmers from Somalia to the Sudan. They often devour every stick of greenery along their flight path. Some swarms have been reported to be up to forty miles wide and sixty miles long.

A geologically young body of water, the Gulf of Aden measured 480 nautical miles in length with varying widths of up to 175 miles across. The two sides of the Gulf were somewhat similar. Somalia's Guban plains were sloped, rocky, and barren. Along the Gulf of Aden's northern coast, Yemen was equally barren in its own way—less rocky, but equally dusty and offering little in the way of visual variety. After months of staring out at open waters, the crew longed to see something quite different. Both sides of the Gulf of Aden answered that longing, but perhaps not in exactly the way they envisioned.

The Gulf offered an assortment of fresh fish. This had not been true crossing the ocean. The crew managed to catch a barracuda or a tuna-like fish every time they tossed their lines over the side. After taking pictures of their prize catch, Paul prepared the fresh fish for dinner—a welcome variety to their menu. It didn't matter that they weren't exactly sure what they were eating; it was delicious!

Red Sea fishing—the best ever! Steve with barracuda

After three days of sailing, the crew sighted the Aden Peninsula and its lighthouse. On August 14 they entered the outer harbor and signaled the control tower. Within minutes, a harbor pilot boarded the *Suzy Wong* and guided them into the inner harbor. The crew had arrived in Arabia.

CHAPTER 32

THE ARABIAN PENINSULA

In Aden, the crew made contact with the British military command and returned the emergency homing device lent to them when departing from RAF Gan in the Maldives. As in most of the ports they visited, word of the *Suzy Wong*'s arrival preceded them. The boat had achieved certain renown, especially in British-controlled countries. This celebrity status brought the crew some luxurious amenities they would otherwise not have had. There were invitations to high-level British officers' homes, and parties hosted by the United States Consul General's office.

The first of such social occasions in Aden was to begin at 6:30 p.m. the first day after their arrival. Because of the hour, the crew assumed dinner would be served—but the evening dragged on and on with no food. Finally, at 11:00 p.m., it was time to leave and the Americans were starving. A portable fish-and-chips wagon had set up shop down by the dock where the boat was moored. That night the crew was very thankful for this British comfort food.

The following evening they were invited to another home. Being quick to learn, the Americans didn't want to go hungry a second night in a row, so they stopped at the fish-and-chips wagon to stuff their bellies before arriving at the party at 6:30 p.m. Waiters and bartenders were serving drinks and it looked to be the same kind of party as the night before—that is, until the guests sat down to an elaborate eleven-course dinner. The hosts couldn't understand the apparent lack of appetite of their guests of honor.

In a letter to Mary, Paul wrote about the social whirlwind:

> Since my last letter we have been to dinner at someone's house just about every night and up early the next morning working on our *Suzy*. Boy, am I beat. Last night we had a party aboard for all

the service military yachting types. Wednesday night we will have one for everyone else we have met. The English people have been so good to us; not only have they asked us to stay with them and invited us for dinner, but the amount of help we have received in obtaining parts and repairing *Suzy* has been fantastic. When we do get to an area where we have to pay for things again, it will be a real blow.

In the same letter, Paul informed Mary of a message he had received from publicity director, Grady Johnson:

He is arranging a meeting for me with Nancy Kwan (Suzie Wong) when we reach New York City. I wish he could arrange one for me with you right now. He also said that if we arrive in the States in time, Ray Stark, the film's producer, has promised us tickets to the Academy Awards show in March. It has been fun handling the publicity for our trip. I have sure met a lot of interesting people.

At a social gathering at the British Officers' Club, the crew began a lively conversation with two generals. Paul asked if it would be possible to see some of the outlying countryside. The officers said that if the crew was willing to stay over a couple of days, there would be a convoy traveling up-country to the Adenese Protective Levy on the border between Lower Yemen and Upper Yemen, which were at war with each other over territorial rights. When the Americans expressed their interest, the generals arranged for them to travel to a desert outpost near the border called Dhala. They would have to travel in an armed convoy as guests of the British Military, the only possible way for Americans to travel so far outside of the protective enclave of Aden.

The British generals explained that there might be dangers involved in going to the border. Having braved the ocean and Mother Nature, the sailors weren't concerned. There had not been any trouble in quite some time, except for Arab rebels taking occasional pot shots at the British convoys, like the one in which they would be riding.

When the day arrived, the convoy left Aden at 0530h and drove for the first five miles or so on paved roads until the pavement turned into dirt trails. The convoy procession stopped once to wait for a truck repair. The convoy had roughly thirty armored cars, trucks, and Land Rovers. The Americans rode in the second car with the convoy commander. He had only two weeks left to serve in Aden so he could have cared less about formality. Though the distance was less than a hundred miles, it took nine hours by truck across an arid, parched, and dusty plain and up a rocky riverbed to a high plateau.

Upon arriving at Dhala, the Americans saw in the distance a village of windowless, flat-roofed, two-story stone houses with smoke rising out of their upper floors. It was 2:30 p.m. on a hot afternoon and the Americans were caked in dust, their backsides feeling the effect of the bumpy ride. After taking a hot shower and catching a couple hours of sleep, the men felt revived.

The camp was impressive for an outpost in such a remote place. At an elevation of roughly 5,000 feet, it was situated on a small plateau in the rugged mountains. Both British and Arab troops were garrisoned there in tents.

Mountaintop British-Arab military encampment; Dhala, Aden

The Americans were particularly impressed with the discipline and sharpness of the Arab soldiers, who really seemed to love this type of life. Most Arabs wanted to carry a gun but couldn't afford to buy one, so they joined the army and were issued one. They were there by choice. To the sailing crew, it seemed like a French Foreign Legion movie. Someone beat on a drum in the background and the Arab soldiers went through a marching drill that looked like some kind of tribal dance.

Suzy crew with turbaned Arab troopers; Dhala, Aden

The crew stayed two nights in Dhala enjoying their visit. To spare them the bumpy return road trip, the Royal Air Force sent a small propeller-driven two-engine plane to fly them back to Aden. The plane was a Canadian Beaver aircraft with extended wingspan that enabled it to operate safely in high altitudes and on short runways. In Dhala, a plane could only make a landing approach to the dirt runway from one direction because a mountain rose sharply on the other side of the landing strip. The opportunity for a pilot to take a second pass at landing his plane was limited. Knowing this ahead of time made an already harrowing flight even more frightening.

Accompanying the Americans back to Aden was an Arab woman who had fallen and broken her hip. She probably had never seen an airplane before, much less traveled in one. For several days she had been carried on a homemade wooden litter to the British camp for help. From there, the Brits flew her, along with the crew, back to a hospital in Aden.

On August 27, Paul again wrote to Mary:

> We are leaving in the morning for Port Said. As I told you before, the Red Sea will be a rough trip. I don't know how long it will take. We came back yesterday by RAF plane. It only took thirty-five minutes from Dhala to Aden—what a difference. I was busy all day getting supplies for *Suzy* and then we went for a ride on an RAF crash boat. Boy, what speed. Forty knots! Tonight a general called to ask if there was anything he could do. I told him that everything was done and ready, except for picking up the fresh vegetables in the morning. He said he would be there at 8:30 a.m. to drive us around. What a life!

Sailing up the Red Sea would be the greatest challenge the crew had to face so far. It was a 1,100-mile-long narrow body of water, littered with potentially dangerous reefs. They would be traveling directly against the wind, the ever-blowing dust would limit visibility, and the heat would be oppressive. Worst of all, the Red Sea was a very busy sea lane with cargo ships, luxury liners, freighters, and oil tankers passing at all hours of the day and night.

The crew had hoped to find a military ship to carry the *Suzy Wong* up the Red Sea as deck cargo, but even the combined efforts of the Royal Army, Navy, and Air Force couldn't manage it. The Brits had a combined transportation service, and pressure was brought from all sides to have them transport the *Suzy Wong*. But the British captain had the last word, and it was, "No!" The *Suzy Wong* would have to sail the entire length of the Red Sea without assistance.

Chapter 33

The Blowtorch

On August 28 at 1130h the log read, "Cast off RAF Pier bound for Port Suez with four normal crew members aboard." The boat sailed west out of Aden to the Bab-el-Mandeb Strait, which separates the Gulf of Aden from the Red Sea. The wind direction was into the crew's faces and the water temperature at times exceeded ninety degrees. There was no telling how hot the air temperature was. The guys felt as if they were in an oven.

A few days later, on September 2, there was little to no wind so the crew had to motor for a long stretch. As the day continued, the engine started vibrating severely and they had to shut it down so it wouldn't shake apart. Luckily, the next day a good southwest wind came up, filling the sails and putting them back on course. George and Walt worked on repairing the engine with little success, so later that day, when the winds died down, the boat was simply drifting once more amid the massive vessels steaming past them on the busy waterway.

The engine continued to be a problem for the next several days. It would run normally for a while, but then heat up again and begin vibrating. With little to no wind since the previous day, they were drifting off their course, making the humid nights and boiling hot days interminable. Midday on September 6, George and Walt solved the engine's overheating problem by fixing a stopped-up silencer that had been the culprit. Working on the engine in a pitching sailboat in the heat of the day was no easy task.

On September 7 the crew tied up at Port Sudan, roughly one-third of the distance up the Red Sea. As usual, while the Americans were in town, their celebrity status attracted attention. A local radio station interviewed Walt. The interviewer asked him, "What was it like coming up the Red Sea?" Walt replied in his Tennessee twang, "It was like tacking up a blowtorch with somebody throwing sand in your face."

On the next day, September 8, Paul wrote to Mary:

> We arrived in Port Sudan yesterday afternoon. This is just a short
> stop for fuel and water. We will leave for Port Said tomorrow. The
> trip up the Red Sea has been slow and most uncomfortable. Not only
> have the current and wind been against us, but the combination of
> dust from sand storms and heat have made it really grimy. The dust
> just floats on the water.

In Port Sudan, Steve hopped off the boat to get a weather report. He noticed
a Spanish ship in the harbor that had just come down the Red Sea. Steve
befriended the captain and then invited him and his first mate to visit the *Suzy
Wong* and meet her crew. After shooting the breeze for a while, they all decided
to have dinner together aboard the Spanish ship since the captain had a cook.
However, when the Americans arrived for dinner, they found that the cook
had already left for the evening. Paul, being the skilled master of shipboard
cuisine, jumped into action and cooked dinner for everyone. The improvised
meal included beef stew and a cheese omelet as a side dish.

It was in Port Sudan that the crew had their first unfortunate experience
with the police. Walt tried to buy a pack of cigarettes with an American dollar
bill, having no idea that this was illegal. One young Sudanese military officer
summoned the police, who then took Walt to jail. After much discussion with a
lot of miscommunication, the crew managed to convey that they were ignorant
of the law and didn't mean to commit any offense. The authorities weren't
buying it, so Walt stayed in jail. The British harbormaster, a holdover from
the days of British port authority control, finally helped to spring Walt loose.
When it came time for the *Suzy Wong* to depart, the harbormaster conveniently
looked the other way.

On September 10 *Suzy* left Port Sudan with all crew aboard, safe and sound.
George, Steve, and Paul were glad to leave and happy to have Walt out of jail
and reunited with them. They continued their journey tacking up the Red Sea
toward Port Suez and the Suez Canal. Although the weather was still miserably

hot and humid, consistent winds made sailing easier and decreased the effect of the oppressive humidity, much to the delight of crew and dog. Fishing in the Red Sea continued to be a boon. Steve caught a barracuda and Paul cut it into huge pieces and cooked them for breakfast making everyone, including Gou, happy.

Despite the good fishing, the voyage northward up the Red Sea was uncomfortable. Not only was it hot most of the time, but Paul was also having severe stomach pains that incapacitated him for prolonged periods. At one point he was on the cabin floor writhing in agony. With the crew having almost no medical knowledge, they could only watch helplessly and hope that Paul would overcome whatever problems were afflicting him. He still functioned as a working crew member in any way he could because all hands were needed for the Red Sea passage.

In order to beat their way northward against the wind, the men had to tack constantly, crossing the Red Sea six or eight times in any twenty-four-hour period. It was a busy sea lane, where up to 150 ships crossed their path day and night. The *Suzy Wong* might have managed five knots on average, while the other ships traveled at fifteen to twenty knots. Therefore, the larger ships would come upon the smaller boat suddenly, being unable to spot the *Suzy Wong* through the dust and the haze, and just narrowly miss hitting her.

The crew's secret weapon for dealing with this potentially dangerous situation at night was the car headlight they had purchased in Singapore and hooked up to the boat's battery. Whenever they spotted a potential collision, they would shine the headlight at the oncoming ship and then onto their boat's large white sails. The *Suzy Wong* had the legal right of way, being a sailboat, but the crew decided not to play chicken with any supertanker, ocean liner, or freighter. The Americans couldn't run the risk that an approaching ship might not spot them in the dark or in the haze hanging over the Red Sea. Fortunately, the headlight worked like a charm, helping them avoid many such potential collisions.

On the way to Port Suez, the crew encountered rough sea conditions. On September 17 the log read, "Wind & seas have built to near the worst seen so far on the voyage…Double reefed the main, put up the storm jib & set course for the Akhaween lighthouse—called the Brothers Light for the type of parabolic lens used to amplify the intensity of the light." By September 20, the crew had to contend with strong northwest winds blowing at forty to fifty knots. With many ships passing them, the *Suzy Wong* had to navigate in only the short width of the Red Sea near the El Ashrafy Light at the mouth of the Gulf of Suez. Luckily, dawn on September 21 brought a break in the winds. They were still gusting, but not as badly as the crew had been experiencing for days. They were almost to Port Suez.

CHAPTER 34

THE SUEZ CANAL

The *Suzy Wong* arrived in Port Suez at the south end of the Suez Canal on September 22. Immediately they began investigating ways to get through the canal. To their great horror, the crew learned that the cost of passage was approximately $5,000 for a small-sized freighter. They could think of no way to come up with this amount of money. They feared that they would have to backtrack for weeks, having to sail south through the Red Sea, back through the Gulf of Aden, around treacherous Cape Guardafui once more, and southward along the entire length of the African continent.

The Suez Canal had always been a source of worry for the crew. Six months prior to their arrival at Port Suez, they learned that an American sailing yacht had been denied access to the canal and had to turn around and travel south around Africa in order to sail to America. A longshoremen's strike in the Port of New York City had delayed the departure of the *Cleopatra*, an Egyptian cargo ship, so it was assumed that the Egyptians were getting even by refusing passage to the American yacht.

In discussing their immediate problem with others, someone suggested that they contact a young Egyptian gentleman who worked for an American company that serviced US ships going through the canal. The crew quickly sought him out and asked him what he would suggest they do. The Egyptian said, "It will take a few days, but I think we can work something out. In the meantime, why don't you hire my brother Abdul with his taxi and all of you go see the sights of Cairo?" This suggestion seemed like an extravagance. Here they were, trying to figure out a way to pay for their canal passage. The idea of sightseeing was just one more expense they couldn't afford.

Despite money concerns, everyone was eager to see Cairo. The guys left Gou on board the boat with food and water, hired Abdul's Taxi, and piled into the cramped car for the long ninety-mile cab ride into the city. They had negotiated a fare that included the driver, a guided tour of the famous landmarks, a cheap hotel, and a return trip the next day.

During their whirlwind tour, the Americans went to the National Museum. It was a huge repository of treasures that normally required more than two full days to properly visit, but they only had a couple of hours. From there Abdul drove them to Giza, about ten miles from downtown Cairo, to see the Pyramids and the Sphinx.

Paul smiles with inscrutable Sphinx; Cairo, Egypt

It must have been 110 degrees in the sun, so they climbed inside one of the massive pyramids and got to the center where the heat of the day couldn't penetrate. Taking in the size of the structure, they estimated that each of the stones was the height of a man. The Americans were awestruck contemplating how the ancient Egyptians had managed to build these colossal structures without modern-day equipment.

Finally, the cab took them to see the Citadel in Old Cairo and some of the city's surrounding neighborhoods. It turned out to be a fantastic trip; certainly a highlight of their voyage so far. They concluded it was well worth it, despite the exorbitant price of ninety-eight dollars total for all four men.

Upon their return to Port Suez, the Americans again went to see the helpful Egyptian gentleman. He had sorted everything out for *Suzy*'s canal passage. The Egyptian government had agreed to let the Americans go through the canal with the *Suzy Wong* being classified as a private yacht. The only monetary charge was a recording fee of 1½ British pounds sterling, or about $5.50.

The crew had no idea why they had been given this deal, and no one bothered to enlighten them except to say that there were two conditions attached: First, the government required that a pilot be on board at all times for the two days it would take to traverse the canal. There would be no charge for the pilot's services, but the crew would need to provide all meals. The pilot could either eat with the crew or bring his own food at the crew's expense. The second condition for the canal passage was that the *Suzy Wong* be inspected and written up by an Egyptian customs official. The crew was more than happy to agree to these conditions.

The inspector came aboard and began measuring everything on the boat, including the little drawers where toothbrushes were kept. Each crewman offered a silent prayer that he wouldn't find the stash of weapons. Instead, he said, "You have too much alcohol on board."

Paul replied, "Would you like to have some?"

"No. I'm a Muslim." He added, "Your food supply is also over the allotted amount."

Paul explained to him that their voyage would continue around the world and the food onboard was necessary for their many months of remaining travel. With exasperation, Paul asked, "What should we do?" The inspector's reply was strange, since he was in charge of making the report. He said simply, "If I were you, I would say nothing." And that is exactly what they did.

The *Suzy Wong* was finally ready to begin her journey through the Suez Canal when the presiding official asked, "Where is your Egyptian flag?" The resourceful Egyptian gentleman who had arranged this swell deal for the Americans came through for them once again by producing a small 5 x 3½-inch flag that he had taken from his own desk. Though hardly visible from more than a few feet away, the tiny flag flying from the mast would satisfy the officials as the *Suzy Wong* passed through the Suez Canal.

On September 25 the *Suzy Wong* entered the Suez Canal as recorded by that day's log entry at 1130h. Going through the canal was a slow process for *Suzy*. Her little engine generated a maximum speed of only four knots while the larger ships traveled at seven knots. The small boat couldn't keep up, so she was assigned to follow at the end of the northbound convoy. All the drawbridges had to be opened to allow for the boat's fifty-five-foot mast.

Observing traffic in the Suez Canal

The Americans couldn't make the trip through the canal in one day because their slower boat would interfere with the next northbound convoy. The first evening they anchored in the Great Bitter Lake, thirty-four miles (halfway) through the canal. They continued to Port Said the next day.

During the passage, conversations with their pilot (who happened to be Greek) revealed his opinions about the canal management. He felt the Egyptians were doing a far better job of running the canal than the British had ever done. This was news to the Americans and probably would have been news for the Egyptians and the Brits as well.

One day the air temperature exceeded one hundred degrees Fahrenheit with not a whisper of a breeze. Being at the helm, Steve was the captain in charge for this leg of their voyage. The dinghy was in the water behind the boat. Since it usually rode on deck, Captain Steve gave the order to haul in the dinghy. This job required two men, so Paul asked George to help him. George thought it was too hot to exert the effort and replied, "The dinghy doesn't need to come in."

Trying to keep the peace, Paul said, "Steve, do you really need the dinghy brought in?"

Captain Steve said, "Yes, I really do want the dinghy pulled aboard!"

Paul turned to George and said, "Hey, Steve is the captain and he wants the dinghy in."

George said, "Screw Steve, it's too damn hot!"

Paul shot back, "Okay, the next time you need help, you can just go to hell!"

Hot, tired, and irritable, George and Paul began arguing and almost came to blows when the rope attached to the dinghy suddenly broke, taking the matter (as well as the dinghy) out of their hands. There was nothing for the bickering crew to do but circle back and retrieve the dinghy from the middle of the waterway.

Most times everyone got along, but after months together in cramped quarters, the crew could tell when someone was about to blow his top. They realized that George was simply hot and irritable, and in a short while this blowup was forgotten.

CHAPTER 35

THE MEDITERRANEAN AT LAST

On September 27 the *Suzy Wong* landed in Port Said, the northern exit point of the Suez Canal. The crew stayed just one night to rest before starting the next leg of their voyage. While there, they received two notes from press agent Irving Hoffman. He had sent one note to the crew in care of the American Embassy in Aden, Yemen, but the crew had already left Yemen so the note got forwarded to the American Consulate in Port Said. The note said simply, "Loved your latest report. Keep writing. Return safely to the US. Regards, Old Seadog." The second note was sent directly to Port Said and it read, "Glad the R.A.F. has given you the VIP treatment. Love, Irving." Unlike the correspondence between Paul and Mary, Irving's letters had no numbering system, so Hoffman's comments often seemed amusingly out-of-the-loop.

On the morning of September 28, the Egyptian Police and harbor officials cleared the *Suzy Wong* to leave Port Said. The boat departed its anchorage and headed into the Mediterranean Sea. Turning toward the northeast, the boat sailed up the coast of the Sinai Peninsula and Israel and headed for Lebanon. (The log entry for this date omits reference to Gou being on board, but he was most definitely still part of the crew.)

On the evening of September 29 at 1900h, the log stated, "Positively identified the city to the east as Haifa. Position seven miles NW of the city." They could see the distant light at the top of Mt. Carmel, famous for the cave where Biblical prophet Elijah sought shelter on his journey into the wilderness. They sailed past Haifa, Israel, arriving the next morning in Beirut Harbor where they wandered around the city for a few days checking out the surroundings.

Over many centuries, Beirut developed a reputation as a crossroads between three continents—Europe, Asia, and Africa. Following World War II, tourists flocked to the triangular-shaped city on the eastern edge of the Mediterranean, proclaiming it the Paris of the Middle East for its elegant colonial architecture, broad avenues, and sidewalk cafés. Not only was Beirut an attractive place, it had a far more temperate climate than the Red Sea—still very warm, but cooled by Mediterranean breezes.

As was his custom in every port, Paul made sure to write Mary. In his letter from October 6, he said,

> Tomorrow is your birthday. Many happy returns of the day. I only wish we could be together. I would send you the moon if I could, but for now the best I can do is send you all my love—and I mean ALL just for you, sweetheart.

Unfortunately, Paul was still not in peak form. He had been having excruciating abdominal pain for some time. Several times during the rough last leg of the passage up the Red Sea he couldn't get out of his bunk. He thought he was losing his mind because the pain would come and go. One day it was on the left side of his body, the next day on the right. Checking the medical books they had on board, George and Walt believed that Paul had come down with dysentery. While walking down Beirut's main boulevard one day, Paul doubled over in pain. He blindly started to cross the busy lanes of traffic and managed to make it without being struck by a car. He was in so much pain that he probably wouldn't have cared if he had been run over.

As it turned out, the Commodore of the Beirut Yacht Club, Fred Zebouni, happened to be a medical doctor. He immediately had Paul admitted as his own patient to the hospital where he was the head physician.

Paul was in the hospital for two weeks. Dr. Zebouni believed kidney stones were causing the trouble and X-rays confirmed his diagnosis. Paul had one stone on each side, explaining the roving nature of his alternating pain. He would go on to pass three kidney stones during his hospital sojourn. The coup de grace was that Paul's malady was not only kidney stones. The crew had been correct; Paul was indeed suffering from acute amoebic dysentery. Dr. Zebouni surmised that insufficient water intake at sea had caused these conditions.

Paul had no idea how he was going to pay for his long hospital stay and this caused him considerable anxiety. When he was released, the doctor presented the bill. Surely the doctor had made a mistake, because the balance due was less than forty dollars. "How can this be all I owe?" Paul asked incredulously.

Dr. Zebouni replied, "I put you in the hospital as a colleague."

"But I'm not a doctor!" Paul protested.

"Yes, but we both sail boats." And that was the last the good doctor had to say about it.

The crew of the *Suzy Wong* had also become friendly with John Noble, president of Tapline, the Trans-Arabian pipeline company that was a consortium of many major oil companies. John and his wife met the crew at the Beirut Yacht Club and later invited them to a party at their home. While there, Steve saw a family photograph that looked familiar and asked the Nobles about it. The picture was of their son, who had graduated from Brown University where he was on the wrestling team. Steve had graduated from Yale where he had also been on the wrestling team. It turned out that Steve and the Nobles' son had been wrestling opponents in 1957 during their senior year when Steve had an undefeated record.

After his hospital stay Paul was feeling much better, although he still needed time to recuperate. The Nobles were fabulously wealthy and lived on the entire top floor of a beautiful six-story apartment building with unbelievable views of the harbor and city. They invited Paul to stay with them until he was well enough to travel again. This would be luxury living for Paul, so he planned to repay their kindness by painting all of their outdoor furniture.

Their six-year-old daughter, Edie, reminded Paul of Eloise from the *Plaza Hotel* stories. She was priceless. Her father said to her one day, "The limousine can't take you to school today."

"Then I won't go!" she replied.

"Oh, yes, you will go! In a taxi," the father persisted.

Instead of remaining defiant, she agreed conditionally, stating that she would only go if it was a red taxi. Her father agreed and, sure enough, a red taxi showed up to take her to school.

Every time the crew landed in a new place it was the same old routine of dinners and parties. Consul's offices and embassies would use the *Suzy* crew as an excuse to throw a party or a social function, and the American sailors would inevitably become the guests of honor. Their celebrity status was actually an attractive way to entertain dignitaries from other embassies or upper level military types.

For one such event, the United States Embassy in Beirut threw a party with the *Suzy* crew—and French explorer Jacques Cousteau—as invited guests. The Embassy sent a Lincoln Continental limousine complete with chauffeur to pick up the guys. The crew had always made a big deal about haggling with the local cab drivers to save money, but with a fancy car like this, they didn't feel right claiming poverty.

Since dogs were a great love of the host, the ambassador sent a special invitation for Gou. For this elite occasion, Gou would need a thorough washing, as his naturally white fur had become as dull as dishwater. Three tubes of Prell shampoo and a nearby water hose solved the problem. To top everything off, the guys tied a red bow around Gou's neck. Now he was ready for the party!

When the limousine pulled up to the ambassador's mountainside villa, Gou couldn't wait for a door to open so he jumped through an open window, being the first to officially arrive at the party. Then, almost immediately, he got into a fight with one of the ambassador's dogs. One of the dogs urinated on a King Louis XIV chair. The ambassador learned an important lesson—don't let your party go to the dogs.

In the midst of his convalescence, Paul felt well enough on one particular day to join Steve on a drive into eastern Lebanon. They traveled fifty miles northeast of the city to the famous temple of Baalbek situated high up in the fertile Bekaa Valley. These Roman ruins are considered among the most extraordinary and enigmatic holy places of ancient times. Long before the Romans conquered the site and built their enormous temple of Jupiter, even before the Phoenicians constructed a temple to the god Baal, Baalbek stood as the largest stone block construction found anywhere in the entire world.

Back in Beiruit, Paul relaxed and the crew worked on the boat between parties. One day Paul was shopping at the souk (open-air marketplace in Muslim countries) and haggling with a saleslady over the price of a bag of apples. Just as he took a bite of a delicious red apple, he suddenly remembered that his doctor had forbidden him to eat any roughage. He wasn't allowed to swallow even a bite of the apple, so he abruptly spit it out. Misunderstanding his reasons for doing so, the saleslady immediately dropped the price by forty percent.

Beirut was such a pleasant break in their journey that George, Walt, and Steve had no problem with extending their stay while Paul recuperated. But it was soon decided that they couldn't wait forever. With Paul out of the hospital and safely ensconced with the Nobles, the other crew members decided they had to go on without him. Paul would stay in Beirut until he was well enough to resume sailing with his buddies.

Paul received a letter dated October 21, 1960, from Irving Hoffman, who was now home in Manhattan. Hoffman wished him a quick recovery and mentioned his anticipation about the opening of the movie, *The World of Suzie Wong*. Irving wrote, "Sorry you were laid low by illness. Hope you recover sufficiently to get to meet the rest of the crew again in Spain. The movie opens at Radio City Music Hall shortly, and I will send you the reviews if you give me your mailing address for late November. I will see a preview next week." Hoffman signed off with the little cartoon figure that had become his personal signature and added, "Here's to your good health!"

Due to construction delays, weather complications, illness, bureaucratic snafus, and the time it took to sail the huge distances from one port to the next, the crew's sailing schedule kept getting pushed back. It had been their original intention to sail the Mediterranean during the summer, but that season, sadly, was already over. At this time they were at least six weeks behind their original plan to be safely across the Atlantic before the hurricane season set in. On October 19, the *Suzy Wong* departed Beirut harbor bound for Tobruk, Libya.

CHAPTER 36

THE AFRICAN COAST

The *Suzy Wong* could have exited the Suez Canal and headed due west along the coast of North Africa in a fairly direct course to Tobruk, Libya. They had planned to sail along the Mediterranean's southern coast near Africa, knowing that the sophisticated European cities on the northern coast would be too expensive for them. But the crew also knew that Paul would most likely find better medical care in the European-style city of Beirut than in some remote outpost along North Africa.

Their Beirut layover had lasted two and a half weeks. Now it was necessary to cut across the lower Mediterranean to get back on track to reach their next destination of Tobruk, Libya. As the crow flies, the distance between Beirut and Tobruk is nine hundred nautical miles, so the crew would be at sea for more than a week.

Almost immediately after clearing Beirut Harbor on October 19, the wind from the west reached Force 6, requiring a shortened sail. This allowed little headway against the elements. For two days the wind worked against the small boat until the weather finally turned in their favor, making for much easier sailing conditions.

On October 26 at 0800h, the crew sighted the north shore of Africa. As they were entering Tobruk Harbor, a small powerboat approached the *Suzy Wong* with a British officer waving to indicate he wanted to talk to the Americans. Pulling alongside their boat, he handed them a Libyan flag to fly from their mast. From his residence overlooking the harbor, the local magistrate would have been extremely annoyed if a visiting craft did not respect his country by flying the Libyan flag. The crew was grateful for the diplomatic tip. In the early afternoon the boat finally entered Tobruk Harbor and anchored stern-to at the RAF Marine Craft Pier.

Tobruk is a protected deep-water harbor and possibly the best natural port along the North African coast, with desert on three sides and cliffs to the south forming a natural barricade. A strategic location during World War II, it became the scene of intense fighting between Allied and Axis powers. Its natural features made it a sheltered harbor during storms and even under attack.

At the beginning of World War II the British maintained a military and naval presence in Tobruk, but in a surprise attack in June 1942, the Italians (with Nazi support) captured Tobruk and the many British units stationed there. It wasn't until November of that year that Allied Forces recaptured the port and retained control for the duration of the war.

As a result of all this fighting, the desert landscape surrounding Tobruk had become a graveyard, both literally and figuratively. Countless broken-down armored vehicles lie abandoned and scattered over the area. These remnants would be a bonanza to anyone willing to start a scrap metal industry.

Tobruk was a small city and there wasn't much to do there, so the crew only stayed for two days. In that short time they made good friends with the Brits, took a city tour, and visited what could be called tourist attractions, including the various graveyards outside of town—each reflecting the culture of its fallen. Pondering the fate of the dead soldiers, the crew thanked their good luck that they were not of the age to have taken part in the battle for Tobruk.

Steve, George, and Walt pay respects at British WWII Memorial to the Fallen;
Tobruk, Libya

On October 28, the crew cast off from the Marine Craft Section, honored with a proper "pipe-off" by the Bay Pipers of the Royal Scots Regiment. The bagpipe music made for quite a farewell. *Suzy Wong* headed out and sailed along the coast for a period of one week, covering another six hundred nautical miles toward the capital city of Tripoli in Libya's northwest corner.

CHAPTER 37

TO THE SHORES OF TRIPOLI

George, Walt, Steve, and Gou had several days of nice weather, allowing for good sailing and a relaxed voyage. Time at the helm had to be extended with the absence of Paul.

On November 4 at 1745h, the boat entered Tripoli Harbor, anchoring at the Tripoli Yacht Club. Once again, their celebrity status had preceded them and the Paramount Pictures press junket waited anxiously for their arrival. The *Tripoli Mirror* radio program blared, "*Suzy Wong* is here! Americans on Second Lap of 20,000 Mile Voyage," telling about the three adventurous Americans with their dog.

A rocky strip of land extends into the Mediterranean Sea, curving to the east to form Tripoli's natural harbor. Since seagoing Phoenicians first founded the strategically located city in the seventh century B.C., it has changed hands many times over the centuries, variously ruled by the Greeks, Carthaginians, Romans, Spaniards, French, and Ottoman Turks. By the start of World War II, the Italians hoped to join this long list of conquerors, having already claimed Tobruk as one of their colonies in their relentless quest to make further inroads into gaining control over northern Africa.

As historians will note, Tripoli's long-standing practice of piracy in the early part of the nineteenth century brought it into two conflicts with the United States, known as the Barbary Wars. Europeans referred to northern Africa as the Barbary Coast, a term coined from its Berber inhabitants. Active from the sixteenth century onward, the Berbers raided ports along the southern European coastline to capture Christians and sail them across the Mediterranean for sale to the Arab markets in Africa and the Middle East. The successive wars with the Barbary Pirate States came to an end in 1815 with the release of Christian slaves and a treaty to guarantee full shipping rights to the United States without payment of tributes.

When the *Suzy Wong* pulled into port, Tripoli still had retained much of its diverse historical heritage. Its old walled city was a picturesque jumble of narrow alleyways leading to traditional mosques, homes, and the public houses known as *khans*. The buildings merged the architectural styles of the country's many conquerors, with particularly strong Turkish, Spanish, Maltese, and Italian influences. Situated on a promontory above the city was the spectacular fortress of Assai al-Hamra, also referred to as the Red Castle, which housed a maze of courtyards and buildings.

For the *Suzy* crew, Tripoli was not only a picturesque place to do some sightseeing, but also a cosmopolitan city where they could attend some impressive social events, not the least of which was an invitation to the Marine Ball commemorating the 185th anniversary of the founding of the US Marine Corps.

For many Americans, Tripoli had become synonymous with the marines ever since its inclusion in the Marine Corps Hymn. With music taken from the popular "Gendarmes Duet" from Offenbach's opera, *Geneviève de Brabant*, the hymn begins:

> From the Halls of Montezuma
> To the shores of Tripoli
> We fight our country's battles
> In the air, on land and sea.

The line "To the shores of Tripoli" refers specifically to the First Barbary War, which was a crucial part of the city's maritime history. The Americans felt as if they were experiencing its living history firsthand.

One day the crew took a trip some eighty miles east of the city along the Mediterranean coast to visit Leptis Magna. This ancient citadel was once a prominent city of the Roman Empire. It has been told that ships arrived in the harbor there during the second century B.C., bringing water and marble from Italy. Emperor Hadrian built enormous public baths, which became the social hub of the city. Ornate mosaics had, at one time, adorned the walls of these bathhouses.

Once-spectacular Leptis Magna, ruins of a Roman City; Libya

A large amphitheater sits wedged into a hillside above Leptis Magna and its sheer size (capacity 20,000) hints at the once-prominent position the city held within the Roman Empire. Its grandeur, however, was not instantly apparent to the visiting crew. It looked much like an old ghost town in the American West. Most of the city was hidden, buried by centuries of desert reclaiming its land after its citizens had abandoned it. In 1960, most of Leptis Magna still sat silently beneath the sands, waiting for history to rediscover it.

During their stay in Tripoli, the crew enjoyed watching the people stroll down the streets and boardwalks. The local men seemed to be dressed in their Sunday finest, probably hoping to attract the attention of the lovely ladies also out for an afternoon stroll.

The crew met William Cramer, a US Marine and veteran of the Korean War. He was still in peak physical condition and expressed an interest in crewing the next leg of their voyage. With Paul still convalescing in Beirut, the guys were glad to have a replacement, so they invited Bill to join them. On November 15 at 1310h, the log read, "Cast off from Tripoli Yacht Club bound for Bizerte, Tunisia, with Banks, Jackson, Todd, and William A. Cramer as a working crew member aboard." Gou, of course, was there too.

Chapter 38

Rough Weather

Just three hours outside of Tripoli Harbor, Steve Jackson became the first man overboard. The crew was getting ready to raise the mainsail when a large wave made the boat lurch sideways. Steve's weight fell against the boom, causing the topping lift (rope from the mast top that supports the boom's outer end when the mainsail is down) to break. The boom fell, knocking Steve over the side. He shuddered at the thought of their first man-overboard drill in the Indian Ocean and was glad to have caught hold of the safety lines, thus avoiding the tragic fate of the seat cushion that was never again seen.

Steve quickly scrambled back on board. He had gotten the wind knocked out of him, but sustained no injuries. The end of the boom was not so fortunate. The dingy that rested on the cabin roof just under the boom had served as a fulcrum, causing the boom to splinter where it attached to the mast. The men were now on a sailboat that couldn't use its mainsail. George and Walt had to figure out a way to jury-rig the sail without a proper boom.

With the boom out of action and the mainsail unusable, putting into Malta seemed like a good idea. Malta had a British naval base where the crew could reconnect with some Brits they had recently met while touring Leptis Magna in Libya and perhaps enlist some help with the repairs. The four men sailed the two hundred nautical miles to Malta using the Genoa jib and mizzen. Luckily, the wind was on their beam and remained steady the entire way, effectively pushing them straight toward the island.

Upon entering Malta's Grand Harbor on November 18, the forty-one-foot *Suzy Wong* came upon the enormous USS *Nautilus*, America's first atomic submarine, which was anchored in the middle of the harbor. The crew later learned that the *Nautilus* was on a goodwill mission and was not allowed to pull alongside the pier for safety and security reasons. The *Suzy Wong* crew was so fascinated by the sub that they circled it once to get a close-up look before heading to the shipyard for repairs.

USS *Nautilus*, America's first nuclear-powered submarine; Valletta, Malta

Malta was a beautiful place. Almost all of its older buildings were fortresses dating back to about fifteen hundred B.C. Ancient ruins and old castles covered the island. There was much to see, but even more for the crew to do before going sightseeing. They reconnected with their British friends who once again came through for the Americans and assisted in repairing the broken boom.

The sailing season was growing shorter by the day, so they couldn't afford to stop in Malta for long. The Mediterranean was known for sudden storms at that time of year. Common sense won out over the desire to relax and play tourists for a few extra days.

By November 21, repairs were finished and the crew was ready to set sail again, this time bound for Bizerte, Tunisia, and then on to Mallorca, Spain, before attempting to cross the Atlantic Ocean.

Starting out from Malta, sailing conditions were excellent through the end of the next day. Then the wind changed to the northwest and its velocity increased. The log on November 22 at 1600h read, "Sighted Cape Bon Light. The NW wind has reached gale force. We are beating to the north with storm jib and mizzen."

The following day, the passage from Malta to Tunisia suddenly became turbulent, which is typical of sailing in the Mediterranean during autumn. The storm blew in from the Atlantic as their boat approached Tunisia. They were sailing in a near-calm sea, having just finished dinner as the sun was setting in the west. Within twenty minutes, winds of near-hurricane force buffeted the boat. By noon the next day, winds remained heavy with gusts up to fifty knots. The windblown seas made sailing almost impossible.

Since they were close to Cape Bon off of Tunisia, the crew decided it was safest to sail in a back and forth pattern and wait for the storm to subside. It amounted to marking time at sea with minimum sail area exposed to the strong winds. Day and night they would tack out toward the isle of Sicily and then back toward Cape Bon, more or less holding their position. The seas were turbulent the entire time, and the crew was never able to dry off. The storm lasted three full days.

Their new crew member, Bill Cramer, was absolutely miserable! A marine, Bill was a tough guy and strong as an ox, but he couldn't handle the motion of the boat. He was sick for almost the entire trip. Steve could sympathize with Bill, having been seasick himself the first three days out of every port for the first half of the voyage. Eventually, Steve had gotten his sea legs, but poor Bill never did. After just a few days, Steve was sure this short trip would cure Bill of ever wanting to put to sea again.

Finally, on November 25, after what seemed much longer than three days, the winds trailed off and the barometer started rising. At 0700h, they were twenty miles northeast of Cape Bon under a reefed main and jib. Eleven hours later, they passed the cape to the north with just twenty-five miles left to reach Bizerte, Tunisia. They were fortunate not to have sustained any significant damage from the storm. It still took them another day and a half before they arrived in Bizerte Harbor and secured their boat to the municipal pier. With the exception of tempest-tossed Bill, the crew members were in good shape; they just needed to rest and dry out.

The Americans celebrated a belated Thanksgiving in Bizerte, having missed the holiday while riding out their stormy crossing from Malta. Someone had given them canned chicken while they were in Tripoli, so they served that for their Thanksgiving dinner. The meal was fine for the starving crew, but at times like these they missed Paul and his culinary skills.

Their stay in Bizerte was made more enjoyable by the camaraderie they formed with a group of French Army and Navy enlisted men who showed them around town. The French spoke poor English and the Americans spoke poor French, so their interactions were often comically confused. The Americans invited their new friends on board the *Suzy Wong* for a meal cooked by George and Steve—a feast comprised of fish stew and homemade baked beans. One of the army boys played the guitar, and everyone had a ball singing French and American songs.

Meanwhile, in New York City, it was the season of fall movie premieres. *The World of Suzie Wong* had finished post-production editing six months earlier and Paramount Pictures had spent the summer promoting the movie's upcoming release. On Thanksgiving evening, November 24, 1960, *The World of Suzie Wong* had its world premiere at New York's famed Radio City Music Hall. Stars William Holden and Nancy Kwan were in attendance, along with press agent Irving Hoffman, who had promised to invite the crew of the *Suzy Wong* to this event. Unfortunately, however, George, Walt, Steve, and Paul were still out to sea. They never received an invitation and weren't even aware of the movie's premiere.

After an extended weekend in Bizerte, Tunisia, it was time to push on, but Bill Cramer decided he had had enough and couldn't take another day on board the boat. He had experienced seasickness from the moment he stepped aboard in Tripoli. The crew would miss his friendship, but no one would miss the sound of his constant retching over the side of the boat.

With the crew reduced once more to just George, Walt, Steve, and Gou, the boat set sail for Palma de Mallorca in the Balearic Islands off the coast of sunny Spain. During the next five days the winds made for great sailing, but the crew worried that their engine might be wearing out. On December 5 at 1715h, the *Suzy Wong* sailed into Palma Harbor. Walt made the final log entry for the year at 1945h on the same day, writing, "Dropped anchor and made fast to the Club Nautico Pier." The boat would be wintering in Mallorca, allowing the crew much needed rest and relaxation, as well as time for repairs and maintenance on *Suzy* before setting sail again in the spring.

Suzy parked and secured; Club Nautico Marina Pier, Palma de Mallorca, Spain

Unfortunately, Mother Nature wasn't done with them just yet. Shortly after arriving in Mallorca, another strong storm blew in, from the Alps this time, with winds approaching seventy miles per hour. Even though the *Suzy Wong* was securely tied, the force of the wind against the boat kept pushing it closer and closer to the pier. The crew added several long lines end to end, stretching them across the water to an adjacent pier. For three days the storm rocked the boat mercilessly between the two piers. Unbelievably, *Suzy* sustained no damage. Had the crew encountered one of these serious storms while trying to navigate in shallow waters or near a harbor entrance, they would not have been so lucky.

Chapter 39

Time Apart

Paul had left the *Suzy Wong* to be treated for dysentery and kidney stones back in September when they were in Beirut. His doctor had advised him to take a break from sailing. After an absence of more than two months, Paul was eager to rejoin his friends and crewmates. The plan had been for the crew to reunite in Spain.

One of the members of the Beirut Yacht Club was helping Paul secure transportation to Spain. In the 1960s, many freighters had been configured to accommodate passengers. Unfortunately, the ship that Paul was scheduled to take had been cancelled unexpectedly, so he needed to scramble to make a last minute opening on another ship departing from Beirut.

Paul crammed his belongings into a cardboard box and rushed to the pier to board a Greek ship that charged him only twenty-five dollars to travel across the entire length of the Mediterranean to Barcelona, Spain. The price should have been a tip-off to Paul that this would be no luxury cruise. The steamship *Massalia* took nine days to travel from Beirut, making stops along the way at Port Said, Alexandria, Piraeus, Naples, and Genoa. The only cabin accommodations were dormitory class and deck class, both of a quality less than steerage. The *Massalia* had a medical doctor on board which, by international law, allowed the ship to carry additional passengers. In this case, there were approximately 100 such passengers that embarked and disembarked with the frequency of a commuter train. The food was pretty horrible too, but Paul didn't mind. He had learned to rough it after months aboard the *Suzy Wong* and he just wanted to get back with his shipmates.

After months at sea, Walt, George, and Steve found Palma Mallorca to be a great place for an extended stay. They rented an apartment and lived there for the length of their stay on the island. Prices were dirt cheap, while lively nightlife, Spanish music, and pretty girls abounded.

The sailors found many enjoyable distractions, but none as nice as the girls. The only lady they'd had as a constant companion for all these many months had been the *Suzy Wong* herself—a darned boat. While they had sailed into many ports en route to Spain, most of the destinations were fairly remote. Language barriers, tight living quarters, and their lack of money made it difficult for the guys to score with the ladies. Now, with *Suzy* nestled in Mallorca Harbor, these conditions had changed.

As Christmas approached, the crew prepared to fly to Madrid to meet Paul. They made arrangements for Gou's care while they were gone. A friendly neighbor who lived close to the pier offered to provide him with food and water and a place to sleep. Gou was pretty self-sufficient and had his own schedule and daily rituals. Every morning he got up and walked about a mile to check on the *Suzy Wong*. He would sniff around the boat, pee on the fishermen's nets, and then head back. On his way back, he would stop at Nico's Café where patrons who knew Gou would pay the owner to make the dog a bowl of mild curry. Or perhaps he'd drop by Club Americana if he fancied a hamburger.

Gou also frequented Bar Africa, a restaurant owned by a colorful lady from England named Vera. Vera made great spaghetti and spoke in a wonderful combination of Cockney and Spanish. People were amused just hearing her count aloud, "Ooonooo, dueoo, trays, qwatrows…." Often Gou got his morning meal there, preferring these delicacies to his usual dry dog kibble. Gou was as much a celebrity as the sailors on the *Suzy Wong*. His fans all vied for the honor of buying him a meal.

With Gou settled for the winter, the crew flew off to Madrid to reunite with Paul. Together they descended upon the apartment of Paul's girlfriend, Mary. They spent the afternoon shopping and sightseeing. On Christmas Eve, the four guys squired Mary to a fashionable holiday dinner followed by a Flamenco stage show. Then Mary enlisted the men to decorate her Christmas tree.

After visiting Madrid for a couple of days, the crew said goodbye to one another and headed off in different directions. Being in such close quarters for nearly a year, they needed a break not only from the boat and sailing, but from each other as well. Paul had been corresponding with Mary for nine months and he felt that their relationship was strengthening. Now that he finally had a chance to be with her, Paul wasn't going anywhere.

George and Walt took two trains and a ferry from Madrid to London. Their primary purpose was to see the sights and visit some friends. They also needed to get replacement parts for the engine. They caught a train to Henley and visited the headquarters of Stuart Turner Limited. The owners of the company were happy to receive them and hear about the *Suzy Wong*'s voyage. George and Walt were able to obtain the replacement parts needed to rebuild the engine upon their return to Mallorca. They were charged next to nothing for the parts.

The Stuart Turner owners appreciated all the operational information George and Walter were able to provide about their engine. Not all of it was favorable, as there had been many problems along the way. But they did happen to mention meeting a man at RAF Gan in the Maldives who had once worked for Stuart Turner Limited. This man had left their employment to join the British Army at the start of World War II, was subsequently captured in Singapore, and spent the duration of the war in a Japanese prison camp. The Stuart Turner owners had not heard from him again and assumed he had died. They were most happy to hear of his survival.

Steve traveled to Switzerland and Austria to visit friends and go skiing. On his way to Innsbruck, he met two American girls on the train who were students in Vienna. Not wanting to pass up a potential opportunity, Steve said he might travel to Vienna after skiing and he offered to visit the girls there. They all agreed and said their goodbyes. Then, on the ski slopes, Steve bumped into a former classmate who was accompanying two other American girls. The girls were anxious to find someone to drive their new 220S Mercedes south over the Brenner Pass to Venice, Italy. Steve didn't hesitate to volunteer for that job!

The day before they left for Venice, a third girl joined the group. It took a day and a half of driving over snow-covered mountain roads, with an overnight stop in Trento, to reach their destination. Arriving in Venice, Steve stayed with the girls in an Italian boarding pension in the center of town. After a nine-month dry spell, Steve had a harem all to himself!

Spending time with the girls was a nice change of pace for Steve after being elbow to elbow with three guys on a boat for almost an entire year. Their perspectives and conversations were certainly different and most refreshing. One of the gals even spoke a little Italian. The group stayed together in Venice for three nights, seeing a lot of the city and attending an opera. Steve liked the orchestral music, but he didn't care much for what he considered the operatic caterwauling and wooden acting.

The next day he said goodbye to his companions and their lovely car and the girls continued on their way to Florence and Rome. Writing home to tell his parents about this adventure, Steve imagined that his father never would have understood his decision to bypass the glories of Florence and Rome. Steve, however, found those first two American girls he had met on his way to Innsbruck more alluring. So he took a night train to Vienna, Austria, arriving the next morning. He met up with the girls and together they went sightseeing, ate out a lot, and attended a concert and…another dreaded opera.

In a letter home, Steve wrote of Vienna, "This is the best city so far on the trip. I will leave here on January 22 for Munich and then head for Barcelona and on to Mallorca. Traveling is easy and not expensive when you go by night train with second-class sleeper accommodations."

Chapter 40

Wintering in Mallorca

The crew members were away from each other and the boat for over a month, from Christmas Eve 1960 to the end of January 1961. It was a good break for the sailors, but Gou had really missed them. When the four guys returned to the boat, Gou greeted each one like the other three never existed. He was a most extraordinary shipmate.

Now that their vacation was over, it was time to get back to the work of readying the boat for their Atlantic crossing in the spring. First, they needed supplies. Since Mary DeForest worked at the United States Embassy in Madrid, Paul asked for her help in buying supplies from the Military PX (Post Exchange) at the Torrejon Air Base. The Americans wanted American things like cigarettes, peanut butter, and Spam, among other necessities. Mayonnaise from the United States was also a much sought after commodity. When he first got to Spain, Steve said, "The Spanish may have invented mayonnaise, but then they lost the recipe!" He preferred the taste of the American spread made from vegetable oil, egg yolks, salt, pepper, and yellow food dye. He never could get used to the olive oil, lemon juice, vinegar, and spices found in European mayonnaise.

Mary was happy to shop for the crew at the American PX. She shipped the goods from Madrid to Palma de Mallorca. When the boxes arrived, the customs officials asked the crew what the boxes contained. Paul said, "Oh, just some necessary supplies for the continuation of our arduous ocean voyage." Just to be sure, customs cut a hole in one of the cartons and saw the word "Camel" written on something inside. Cigarettes were hardly a necessity, so they insisted that the crew open all the boxes. With some swift thinking and smooth talk, Paul persuaded the officials to allow them to keep everything on the condition that the supplies were locked in a cabinet on the boat. Customs inspected the storage cabinet and then sealed it securely with their official tape. Thereafter, getting into that cabinet meant removing and replacing the tape as precisely as possible!

Their remaining days in Mallorca were filled with long hours of hard work. Walt and George overhauled the Stuart Turner diesel engine using the replacement parts obtained in England. Paul and Steve set about painting and making other needed repairs. At one point during their refurbishment, the crew had *Suzy* hauled out of the water in order to repaint the ship's bottom and refinish the enameled sides. In the evenings the guys relaxed, tossed down a few drinks at the bar, and chatted with the pretty girls.

George and Walt rebuilding *Suzy's* diesel engine; Mallorca, Spain

Steve took on the difficult, time-consuming job of repairing and refinishing the boat's mast. Most work of this nature should be done with the mast lying horizontal, but in Palma de Mallorca the crew didn't have the means to "unstep" (or take down) the mast. Steve did all this work with the mast in place. He stripped the entire mast—all fifty-five feet of it—and then he re-varnished it. The other crew members had to pull him aloft on the boson's chair at least a hundred times to accomplish this feat.

The guys experienced tremendous personal gratification as the boat gleamed once again. When they were finished, *Suzy* looked as good as when she first slid down the launching ramp in Junk Bay eleven months earlier.

The crew admired many large yachts anchored in the harbor or tied up at the piers in Mallorca. They were particularly impressed with the *Constellation*, a 75-foot schooner that regularly competed in trans-Pacific and trans-Atlantic races. The guys were happy to meet and befriend some of the *Constellation's* crew who were also wintering there in Mallorca.

Another notable yacht was the beautiful 120-foot schooner, *Zaca*. It belonged to Australian-born, American movie star Errol Flynn, who bought it as consolation for his declining career and failing health. He sailed for long periods of time, enjoying his relative solitude on the high seas or in remote ports around the Pacific Rim.

As their four-month stay in Mallorca was coming to an end, the crew realized they had accumulated way too much junk to take with them on the next leg of their voyage. Paul, always serving as *Suzy's* social coordinator, came up with the idea of holding an auction to sell off some of their extra items. The crew decided to hold the auction in the public square next to the yacht club, and then they purchased the necessary permit from the authorities.

On the scheduled day, they were ready to begin their auction when a policeman came up and stood next to them at center stage. They thought he was there for crowd control, but he said it was his job to keep the undesirables away. Despite the undesirables, they auctioned off several items.

Suzy crew throws hilarious auction; Mallorca, Spain

One item on the auction block was a kerosene room heater. As the auctioneer, Paul was trying to demonstrate how the heater operated. Try as he might, he couldn't get that heater to function. Finally, he muttered, "Oh, Hell!" He grabbed a quart of gasoline and poured it on the heater. Then he struck a match and set it on fire. The heater was no longer up for sale!

After the auction, the crew staged an eating competition on the quay. They figured it would be a fun distraction to see Gou go up against two grown men. Instead of using utensils, the contestants would have to plunge their faces into enormous bowls of spaghetti, courtesy of Bar Africa. All the commotion attracted a considerable crowd to this curious event, mostly from the expatriate community. Everyone joined in the festivities. An old fisherman loaned Paul his nets to drape around the lampposts for decorations. The crew supplied the attendees with food and a very large vat of sangria made with cheap wine.

The guys figured Gou would win hands down, as he was famous for sucking down huge bowls of spaghetti in seconds. But Gou got confused when he saw the men on all fours going for the food next to him, so he hesitated. A British fellow from a neighboring boat took the lead and almost won, but then the judges determined he cheated and disqualified him. Gou was declared the winner after all!

After the event, a newspaper article appeared in the local paper that read:

A garishly painted bicycle, odd items of personal clothing, an oil stove, an innocent bystander's car, and five liters of rum were amongst the items that were literally put under the auction hammer outside Club Nautico last Sunday. For the princely sum of 25 pesetas, the crew of the yacht *Suzy Wong* had obtained police permission to hold a public auction in the square outside the yacht club. Nothing like it had ever been seen before in Mallorca and it is extremely doubtful it will ever be seen again!

Although the occasion was hilarious, there was an overtone of sadness because this selling off of surplus stores meant that the yacht, *Suzy Wong*...was now ready for sea and would soon be leaving our port for probably the last time. Since the *Suzy* sailed into port at the beginning of December, having made the long haul from Hong Kong, the four young Americans who are her owners and crew, George Todd, Paul Cardoza, Steve Jackson, and Walter Banks, have made many firm friends on the island.

One of those new friends was Joe Gerardin. He wanted to be part of the *Suzy Wong* adventure like J.D. and Blackie and Bill before him. So they signed him on as a crew member for just the one week it would take to sail to Gibraltar.

On Saturday, April 15, 1961, at 0925, the first log entry for the new year read, "Departed Club Nautico Pier, bound for Gibraltar with Banks, Jackson, Cardoza, Todd, and Joe Gerardin aboard as crew. Cleared harbor. A fair south breeze blowing." (As always, Gou was the onboard dog, but if he wasn't standing beside the person writing in the log, his presence was often not noted.)

CHAPTER 41

COSTA DEL SOL

The mountains of southern Spain loomed large, rugged, and beautiful in the warm Mediterranean sunshine. Sailing was good as the boat proceeded south along the east coast of Spain. Passing the coastal towns of Cartagena and Almeria, the *Suzy Wong* swung west toward Costa del Sol.

Like Bill, the marine from Tripoli who had traveled briefly on the boat, Joe was prone to seasickness. He spent the first few days of his voyage feeling very sick to his stomach. Heaving over the side of the boat, he missed a lot of the lovely scenery. Gradually, he too got used to the rocking sensation of the waves.

On April 20, the boat entered Malaga Harbor and tied up at the customs pier. Steve and Paul soon set out by land for the town of Seville to see the sights. They planned to rejoin the boat in Gibraltar. George, Walt, and Joe continued on to Gibraltar after staying in Malaga for only a few hours.

Steve and Paul happened upon an annual weeklong festival in Seveille. The town was bustling with activity and nonstop parties. Entire families strolled through the town center dressed in ornate, colorful outfits. The guys wondered if and when these people ever stopped to sleep.

Of course, they couldn't visit Seville without taking in a bullfight. So they found the best arena in Spain. The pageantry was simply outstanding. The bullfighters on horseback, called *rejoneadores*, entered with their horses prancing backward on their hind legs. Overall, it was a magnificent spectacle, though the final blow was difficult to watch.

While Paul and Steve enjoyed their immersion in Seville's culture, George, Walt, and Joe found their own entertainment. They motored the boat slowly up the coast while using binoculars to ogle at the girls tanning on the beaches along the way.

On Friday, April 21, Walt wrote in the log, "Entered Gibraltar harbor after standing off for several hours waiting for daylight. Tied up to Berth 40, all secure." At this point, Joe departed the boat and returned to Mallorca as planned. Paul and Steve rejoined the rest of the crew and together they stayed in Gibraltar for the next week. They saw the colony of monkeys that lived up on the great rock and explored the network of tunnels dug underneath it. Mostly, they appreciated the grandness of this gigantic limestone promontory situated off the coast of Spain.

Gibraltar had been a British colony for more than 250 years. The *Suzy* crew loved going to any place that had a strong British presence because the Brits always exhibited an innate appreciation for sailors. Everywhere the crew went, they were welcomed heartily by the Brits, and Gibraltar was no exception. Yet they were keenly focused on the urgent need to cross the Atlantic Ocean ahead of the hurricane season and anxious to be moving on to their next port of call.

The *Suzy Wong* departed Gibraltar on April 27 with her first female crew member aboard. Steve had made the acquaintance of a woman named Evangeline in Mallorca and, enamored with her, invited her to sail with them. Paul didn't care for Evie, dubbing her "an eighteen carat, diamond-studded user and loser." Not wanting to get into a fight with his friend, Steve had no comment.

The boat crossed the Strait of Gibraltar and entered the Atlantic Ocean, sailing down the northwestern coast of Morocco. Two days later, on April 29 at 0605h, they entered Casablanca Harbor.

The movie *Casablanca* had opened almost twenty years earlier, but it still prompted powerful associations for anyone who had seen it. The crew imagined that they were sailing into a port of glamorous intrigue where they might bump into a Humphrey Bogart-type at Rick's American Café. The reality proved far less interesting, as Rick's didn't even exist outside the movie. Had there been such a place, the cash-strapped Americans probably wouldn't have been able to afford its local brew and posh atmosphere.

Steve traveled fifty miles to Rabat, Morocco, to visit his cousin, Ned Schaefer, who worked at the American Consulate and lived in Rabat with his wife, Nancy, and their two boys. Beyond that, the crew didn't do much of anything because they were always on a tight budget. Irving Hoffman apparently had not sent out an announcement to alert the Casablanca press that the *Suzy* crew was on their way. He had either dropped the ball or simply decided to stop promoting *The World of Suzie Wong* since it had already been in the theaters for five months. In any case, this Moroccan city seemed indifferent to their presence. Casablanca would have to remain a movie fantasy for them.

Romance wasn't in the air either, but, alas—Evie was. Steve had put her on a plane! She wasn't a bad sort and the crew (other than Paul) didn't have any particular objection to her; she just didn't fit in with the all-male crew. The boat simply wasn't large enough for such challenges.

CHAPTER 42

GOU DISAPPEARS

The *Suzy* crew departed Casablanca on May 2, 1961, bound for the Canary Islands off the coast of Africa. The first day was tricky because it involved sailing downwind. The breeze was relatively light and often unreliable. At times it seemed the wind stopped completely, so sailing was nearly impossible. But, still, the boat rocked violently from side to side, which made sleeping below deck uncomfortable and difficult.

The *Suzy Wong* sailed the length of the Moroccan coastline until the next morning when the boat began to head west into the Atlantic Ocean. From the time they left the Seychelles Islands, the crew had seen nine months and five thousand miles of African coastline come and go, traveling from Somaliland in the northeast to Morocco in the northwest. Now, as they sailed west toward the Americas, Africa faded from sight behind them.

On the third day, the wind picked up and they had fast sailing using various sail combinations for the remainder of this leg of the voyage. The crew rigged the spinnaker pole to the big Genoa jib and *Suzy* ran downwind making nearly six knots. They dropped anchor in Las Palmas de Gran Canaria in the Canary Islands on May 6, having covered five hundred miles in just four days with little or no help from the engine or an ocean current.

The sailors spent several days preparing for the Atlantic crossing. They worked on the boat, provisioned the galley, and topped off the water and fuel tanks.

On their sixth day in Las Palmas, the crew awoke to find that Gou was missing. They couldn't spot him on the dock, along the beach, or anywhere. They walked along the sand and called out his name, but that didn't bring him running as it normally would have. A thorough search of the small town was unsuccessful as well. It seemed that Gou had run off or been stolen. The crew was horror-struck.

The more they looked without finding him, the more anxious and upset they became. They wondered what to do. If they held up their Atlantic crossing, they might run into the hurricane season. But they also couldn't imagine leaving Gou behind.

Finally, Steve paid a visit to a Spanish radio station and asked them to put out an announcement about the lost dog. The price for a series of ads was ridiculously low (less than five dollars), so he didn't hesitate. The radio announcer gave a description of Gou and pleaded with listeners to contact the owners of the *Suzy Wong* if they spotted him. The announcer played on listeners' emotions by stressing the urgency of finding the dog. The crew, he explained, was about to depart and couldn't bear to lose their beloved mascot.

Gou didn't have a collar or any kind of identification, but the crew hoped his distinctive white fur and black tongue would make him easy to find on the island. At 2200h on the night after the radio announcement, four Spaniards brought Gou back to the ship—freshly washed! The Spaniards had found him about six miles away from the beach where the *Suzy Wong* was anchored. Gou had been doing what all dogs do—he had been led astray by a bitch in heat. George remarked, "He was just out chasing a lady, like any other sailor." The guys were absolutely delighted to have Gou back. The rest of the trip would not have been the same without him.

CHAPTER 43

THE ATLANTIC CROSSING

T hus far in their voyage, there had been only two 2-week long stretches of uninterrupted sailing. The first was almost a full year earlier (May 10–22, 1960) when they sailed from Nicobar in the Bay of Bengal to Trincomalee, Ceylon. The second (August 2–14, 1960) occurred when they sailed from Victoria in the Seychelles Islands, arriving in Aden, Yemen. These two long legs paled in comparison to what lay ahead in their next passage from the Canary Islands to Barbados in the southern Caribbean Sea.

The *Suzy Wong* cleared Las Palmas Harbor in the Canary Islands heading west on May 14, 1961. The sky was cloudy and there was little wind, so the crew cranked up the engine. It promptly overheated, causing much smoke but, luckily, little damage. This was not the most auspicious start for the longest and potentially most dangerous leg of their journey.

Captain George at home on the helm; Western Mediterranean

They had good sailing for the first several days. The winds weren't as steady as they had hoped, but Walter, serving as navigator, estimated they were averaging 130 nautical miles per day. That meant they were sailing at a good rate of speed for their forty-one-foot vessel.

In the middle of the next day, they noticed a mass of floating jellyfish in the water alongside the boat. The jellyfishes' whitish-pink flesh shimmered just below the surface, giving the water an almost waxy sheen. George informed his crewmates that these jellyfish had sails that could be inflated. The other guys had no idea what he was talking about. This information didn't sound reasonable, but no one on board was a marine biologist, so they could only surmise that George was pulling their legs.

Mid-afternoon the next day, while trailing a fishing line, they caught a large Bonita, a darkly colored predatory fish. Each of the guys took turns holding it and trying to guess its weight. Their estimates ranged from fifteen to forty pounds. No matter how big, it made for one fine dinner that was enjoyed by all, especially Gou.

Gou ate pretty much anything put before him except martinis and tomatoes. Steve liked giving him peanut butter every now and then, not because the dog showed any particular fondness for it, but because Steve was amused by watching him try to eat it. The peanut butter would get stuck to the roof of his mouth and out would come Gou's black tongue, licking and lapping ceaselessly.

George had his fun with Gou, too. One day while working his galley duty, George played a trick on Gou. He tossed Gou a piece of fish, which Gou caught easily. (Gou was a good fielder, even in the worst of conditions.) George tossed him another piece of fish, which Gou caught again. But when George was ready to toss a third piece of fish, he quickly swapped it for a slice of tomato. Gou caught it, looked up, and promptly spit it into George's face! By trick or trade, Gou simply wouldn't eat tomatoes.

The reward of sailing on a clear night was being able to see an unimaginable array of stars in the sky. There is, perhaps, no place on earth where the night sky is so magnificently full of twinkling lights as in the middle of the ocean. On rare occasions the crew even witnessed a sunrise on one horizon and, at the very same moment, a moonset on the opposite horizon.

Early one morning just before dawn, they sighted a bright, bluish ball of fire falling from the sky. Its brightness intensified until it suddenly disappeared just above the horizon. The crew had no idea what the object was, but the general opinion among them was that they had just witnessed a meteorite splashing into the ocean. What a thrill! These unobstructed celestial shows were surprising and wondrous.

Winds from the east as the boat moved westward across the Atlantic might sound like a sailor's dream. But, actually, when the wind comes from behind, the boat experiences a sideways rocking, lurching motion. And that's what the sailors were stuck with, day and night. Trying to get a good night's sleep under those conditions was difficult, to say the least. Whether sleeping on deck or below in the cabin, the guys had to somehow brace their bodies against both sides of the boat. Otherwise a series of waves could result in injuries or, at least, some bruising. Consequently, the crew decided to sail an alternating downwind tacking course, first putting the wind to one side and then the other. Since tacking was like zigzagging, it added approximately twenty percent to the total nautical miles to cross the Atlantic Ocean. Luckily, they weren't in a race. Making time didn't really matter; making their lives less miserable did.

Seasickness was a real issue during the journey and each had his own way of dealing with it. Walt and Steve had a propensity for it. Walt would feel miserable for hours and hours and then he'd gradually recover. Steve would go immediately to the rail, upchuck, and get right back to work. George, on the other hand, got seasick just once. He became nauseated during the Atlantic crossing when he went below deck to write letters to friends and the fumes from the alcohol stove permeated the cabin. Paul didn't escape being sick at sea either. He had amoebic dysentery, kidney stones, and, on occasion, an upset stomach. But as far as actual seasickness was concerned, he was blessed with a cast-iron constitution.

On May 20 Steve finished the last of the peanut butter. He would no longer have the fun of watching Gou endlessly lick his chops. But the crew was always impressed by the ways Gou could entertain himself. Sometimes the boat happened to sail through a school of flying fish. A number of them would land on deck only to be pounced upon by a vicious dog waiting for his midday snack.

Life at sea, Gou and Steve; Atlantic Ocean

The humans weren't so easily entertained, however. At sea they were on call nearly twenty-four hours a day—manning the helm, adjusting the sails, navigating, studying upcoming ports of call, cooking meals, and cleaning the galley. The list of tasks seemed endless. Each guy looked forward to his free time.

With a collection of cheap paperback novels, the crew had created a small library in a box. Everyone enjoyed reading in his off-hours. It was pleasant sitting propped up with a cushion, escaping for a little while into an Agatha Christie murder mystery or a spy novel. Occasionally one of the guys would be on deck reading when a sudden rogue wave would splash against the side of the boat, drenching both reader and book. Whenever that happened, the reader would simply hang his book up to dry and reach into the box for a new one.

During port visits the guys sometimes engaged in book swaps, taking their stash of paperbacks to a nearby ship and exchanging them for a load of books they hadn't yet read. A new story was something of a luxury. During one quiet moment on the Atlantic crossing, Steve was reading a book that the rest of the crew eagerly anticipated reading next. At one point Steve jumped up shouting, "Oh, crap!" and threw the book overboard. The others were stunned and demanded to know why he had done it. Steve replied, "You wouldn't have liked the ending."

The guys also slept a lot during the day when they were off duty. It was quite pleasant stretching out on deck in the sun or finding a spot in the shade to take a nap. If they were on duty part of every night, they could catch up on sleep during the day. The fresh sea air made for good sleeping, as long as the seas weren't too rough.

Soon the days started to blend together without much variation in their leisure activities. There were days without much excitement—nothing to do or see except endless sea and sky, mile after mile after unending mile. Each sailor had to find his own way of relieving the monotony.

World-sailor, Paul, helms *Suzy* across Atlantic Ocean

George was the dreamer of the bunch. He had become the man of his family at an early age following the death of his father, so he didn't enjoy many youthful pursuits. He had artistic talent and mechanical aptitude, but he really discovered himself while sailing. Often when on a break, George would sit quietly on deck and just enjoy the view. He loved the water, the rhythmic rolling of the boat on gentle waves, and the stillness and quiet of the open ocean at night. He was content to commune with nature and at one point he became so mesmerized that he thought the fish were talking to him.

Steve brought several cameras on the voyage and became the unofficial photographer. Whenever he had a moment, he grabbed his camera and clicked away. If he was bored, he took pictures of Gou napping on deck or yapping at dolphins. If something happened that Steve found interesting, scary, or funny, he ran for his camera to capture the moment. He was such a shutterbug that often he'd be fiddling with the camera when he should have been helping the others with the work at hand.

Paul may have been the designated chef on the voyage, but there were only so many menu items he could concoct. He spent lots of time in the galley just staring at their provisions, trying to invent new recipes. He was also a jokester with an inexhaustible repertoire of stories, jokes, and card tricks. But mostly, Paul spent his free time writing long letters to Mary and countless postcards to his family, staying connected to the people who were most important to him.

Walter was the tinkerer of the crew. He was drawn to gadgets and machinery and enjoyed studying them until he understood how they worked. Some of his free time was spent looking for things to fix. Unfortunately, he didn't have much opportunity to fool around with *Suzy Wong*'s machinery while they were under sail. Like the others, he read and he slept. At one point out of sheer boredom, Walt made oatmeal cookies. He had to pan-fry them since *Suzy* had no oven. The cookies turned out hideously misshapen, but they tasted pretty good!

On the morning of May 23, the crew decided that, just as something to do, they'd conduct a drill to put up the spinnaker (a sail made from 1,500 square feet of very light nylon material). From a distance the sail resembled a red and white balloon stretching from the top of the mast down to the deck. This sail was particularly effective when *Suzy* was heading downwind with a moderate breeze from behind, as was the case most of the way across the Atlantic. It was tied to a boom that held the lower ends away from the boat to keep the sail filled with air. As the drill progressed, the *Suzy Wong* began rocking wildly from side to side. Much to the crew's surprise, the top of the spinnaker had wrapped itself around the upper forestay, preventing the sail from opening up and making it impossible to be lowered.

Spinnaker flogging in downwind Atlantic swells

Walt had always disliked this particular sail, as it was difficult to fly even in ideal conditions. His initial solution was to cut it down. The other three guys didn't agree. They argued about the problem for an hour, trying to figure out what to do next. Then Paul suggested rolling the sail around and around until it formed into a kind of rope that could be passed over the forestay and set free. True to form, Steve ran for his camera and managed to film the incident for posterity. He caught hell from the other three guys for taking photographs rather than lending a hand.

The drill of putting up the spinnaker was not at all essential to their Atlantic crossing, they had simply intended to pass some time. But it ended up costing the four guys most of the day to untangle and lower the spinnaker from the top of their fifty-five-foot mast. Eventually, the mission was accomplished.

Even with a strong breeze filling the sails and the boat running more or less downwind at six knots, they had to fire up the engine occasionally to keep the batteries charged. They believed that, had they not run the engine at regular intervals, the *Suzy Wong* might have registered a sailing record for a trans-Atlantic crossing for a vessel of its size. But any creditable sailing record, to be counted, had to be done unassisted by engine power.

On June 2 at 1515h the men arrived at their destination, spotting the island of Barbados and entering Bridgetown Harbor later that night. *Suzy Wong* had covered 1,900 miles of ocean in just nineteen days.

CHAPTER 44

BARBADOS

Barbados was a small, heavily populated island in the western North Atlantic, east of the Windward Islands and the Caribbean Sea. It was only twenty-one miles long by fourteen miles wide. The trade winds blow from east to west in this part of the Caribbean, so, like many of the islands in this region, the eastern side of Barbados is windblown and rocky while the western, or lee side, is calm and protected. Bridgetown, located on the southwest of the island, was where the Americans first anchored.

On June 9, after spending several days relaxing in Bridgetown, the four young men sailed their boat north along the west coast of Barbados to the Colony Club. This club was arguably the premier resort in all the Caribbean. Situated on the finest stretch of beach on Barbados' west coast, it was a luxury retreat, a restoration and expansion of a former private colonial mansion.

As it turned out, the delayed start of the *Suzy Wong* voyage back in March of 1960 proved advantageous. Had they departed in January as planned, they would have arrived in Barbados during the high season when "snowbirds" (seasonal tourists) flocked to the Caribbean to escape the cold winters up north. Instead, the crew arrived in Barbados at the start of the summer during low season, meaning cheaper prices and fewer tourists.

They anchored about one hundred yards off the Colony Club. Whenever the crew was ashore, they left Gou behind to guard the boat and wait patiently for their return. If any of the crew called to him from land, Gou would leap from the deck into the water and swim ashore. If anyone other than George, Steve, Walt, or Paul called to him, Gou wouldn't budge; he'd just stare.

As usual, the guys were short of funds, and the perks associated with their celebrity status were dwindling. So peanut butter and crackers would have to suffice. Gou, on the other hand, lived like a king. The owner of the Colony Club had fallen madly in love with Gou. She made sure the beautiful, white Chinese

Chow had plenty to eat, and it was never table scraps. Instead, she served him filet mignon cooked to order. The lady liked Gou so much that she offered to buy him for $500, but the crew was unanimously opposed to parting with their beloved mascot.

The four Americans often thought about ways to bring in a few extra dollars. Since they were cruising in the beautiful Caribbean and rum was cheap, they began offering afternoon cruises. They charged about five dollars per person, which included cocktails on board. It turned out to be a good little business. People couldn't resist the allure of sailing into the sunset on a beautiful, exotically named boat, enjoying refreshments served by four rugged seafarers with a white dog. Unfortunately for the tourists, their hosts managed to keep costs down by conveniently running out of everything but the cheap rum.

The guys were gregarious and flirtatious wherever they went—and Barbados was no exception. But the end of their journey was nearly in sight and, after a welcome break from their long ocean crossing, it was time to say goodbye to their latest new friends. Some of the girls took the *Suzy Wong*'s departure harder than others. As the *Suzy* crew was leaving Barbados, several brokenhearted girls posted a farewell sign on the thatch-roofed raft they called home. Their misspelled kiss-off sign read, "Yankey Go Home."

Paul wasn't the only member of the crew to find romance during the voyage. It was in Barbados that Steve met Pat Ewing, who was on vacation with her friends, Ann and Cynthia. Steve and Pat hit it off immediately and spent two days together in Barbados before the *Suzy Wong* departed. Happily, they agreed to meet two weeks later when the *Suzy* would arrive in St. Thomas.

Chapter 45

The Caribbean

On June 20 the crew pushed off from the Colony Club, departing Barbados and sailing north into the Caribbean. Joining the crew as George's special guest was Pat's friend, Cynthia Cantelon, from Ft. Wayne, Indiana.

The boat stopped at a different island every day. Port Castries, St. Lucia, had more volcanic mountains than most other islands in the Caribbean. Here they saw a beautiful row of stunning royal poinciana trees, which were often called *flamboyant trees* for their vibrant red color and perfectly symmetrical shape. These trees were native to Madagascar, but grew in most tropical climates. Many people considered them the most exquisite flowering trees in the world.

On June 22 the *Suzy Wong* stopped on Pigeon Island, a forty-acre islet with two small peaks and numerous historic forts located in the northern region of St. Lucia. As they continued sailing north, two fishing boats approached the *Suzy Wong* and asked where Martinique was. The Americans told them it was dead ahead. Looking surprised, the fishermen then asked where the *Suzy Wong* was from. When the crew told them their home port was Hong Kong, the fishermen must have thought they couldn't possibly know where they were. So they headed in the opposite direction toward St. Lucia. The crew would never know if the fishermen found their way to Martinique.

The next island stop was Fort-de-France, Martinique, on June 23. Fort de France was one of the Caribbean's major towns, situated on the west side of the island. It was the administrative capital of Martinique, but the city always played second fiddle to its neighbor to the north, Saint-Pierre, which was known for its cultural vibrancy and was affectionately referred to as the Paris of the Caribbean. Fort-de-France, however, had its own charm. The imposing Fort-Royal overlooked the lovely bay whose shore was strewn with picturesque cottages and broad palm-lined avenues. They didn't need to stop here, but the crew wanted to see as much as they could before their journey came to an end.

On June 25 the *Suzy Wong* landed on Les Saintes, the northeast part of a beautiful island chain in the Guadeloupe archipelago. Of the nine islands, only two of them were populated, with a combined population of just 3,000 inhabitants. These people relied solely upon the sea for their economic wellbeing. Their native language was French, although there were some Creole dialects spoken as well. Very few of the locals spoke English.

This quiet fishing village was breathtakingly beautiful. The bay's water was unbelievably clear and several old forts dotted the hillsides of the larger island. The town was a quaint, French settlement where the guys and Cynthia spent the afternoon eating fish, swimming, and making general repairs. The high point of the day came when they launched a box kite from the deck. It flew effortlessly in the breeze and probably would have gone up a thousand feet if their fishing line had been longer.

After dark the boat departed Les Saintes bound for English Harbor, Antigua. Cynthia was proving to be a dedicated and worthy sailor, almost one of the guys. When the winds picked up to thirty-five knots the group decided to bypass Antigua and push directly on to the Virgin Islands. The *Suzy Wong* sailed silently past Nevis Island and St. Kitts on June 26.

On June 27 they passed Saba, the smallest island of the Lesser Antilles and home to the highest peak in the archipelago. It was a favorite place for pirates to hide loot from plundered merchant ships in the seventeenth and eighteenth centuries. The island was also known for its lobsters, rum, dramatic volcanic peaks, lush tropical rain forests, and adventurous history. It had just about everything one would expect of a Caribbean paradise. Unfortunately, the crew could only admire it from afar, as the boat skirted the west coast of the island.

On June 28 the crew sighted the British Virgin Islands. They passed through Round Rock Channel into Sir Francis Drake Passage and from there they set their course for Marina Cay. After a man in another boat told the Americans they wouldn't be able to clear customs at that location, the *Suzy Wong* altered course for Road Town. The boat anchored at 1600h and spent the night in the harbor of the island of Tortola in the British Virgin Islands.

The next day was to be a momentous occasion for the crew of the *Suzy Wong*. At 1010h that morning, the boat crossed out of the British Virgin Islands and into the US Virgin Islands. After nearly sixteen months of sailing, the *Suzy Wong* entered American territorial waters for the first time.

They sighted their first American flag on American soil just before anchoring in Cruz Bay, St. John. It took an hour for them to clear US Customs and Immigration. After a few hours of relaxing on land and catching a bite to eat, the *Suzy Wong* and its crew departed Cruz Bay for the short sail to the harbor at Charlotte Amalie on the island of St. Thomas. The four voyagers anchored the boat and then spent the next two weeks taking in the sights before the final push home.

Steve had made plans to rendezvous with Pat, whom he had first met on Barbados. In Saint Thomas, their friendship deepened into a serious relationship as they explored the island together. On one occasion Steve served up a home-cooked meal on the *Suzy Wong* while the boat was at anchor. It was a pleasant evening and the sound of a steel drum band floated across the water from the nearby yacht club. George, Walt, and Paul had conveniently exited for the evening, but Steve wasn't entirely alone with Pat. Gou was there, looking adorable and being very well behaved, giving Steve a lot of competition for Pat's attention.

After dinner Pat, Steve, and Gou came ashore to enjoy dancing at the Yacht Haven Club just as the band was wrapping up for the evening. The couple inquired as to where there was another place to dance, so the band members invited Pat, Steve, and Gou to accompany them to their next gig. After an hour of dancing there, that engagement also ended. The band members then invited the couple to a third venue some distance away. The trip took about an hour; they drove through the mountains in the back of one of the band members' Nash Rambler convertible. Steve wondered if they were being kidnapped. It was already 2:00 a.m. when they all ended up in a small French dance hall where the locals were dancing up a storm. Pat and Steve were the only white people there, and they were certainly the only ones to have brought their dog along.

Pat, a pert blonde and a southerner from Louisville, Kentucky, became the most sought-after dance partner in the hall. Steve's new girlfriend seemed totally at home in this environment. She was having a wonderful time dancing with people she didn't even know. This was the moment Steve realized he was falling for Pat, a gal he had met by chance only a few weeks earlier. After a night of dancing, Steve escorted Pat back to her small hotel well after sunrise.

Chapter 46

The Final Push

The boat departed Yacht Haven, St. Thomas, in the US Virgin Islands at 1720h on July 15, 1961. The next few days held favorable winds and smooth sailing. July 19 was, according to the log, "a dull day except for Paul's sugar cookies, which he cooked on top of the stove. They were enjoyed by all, even if they did look like pancakes."

The boat's radio picked up the first American broadcast station from Miami on July 20 at 0800h. A while later they received a weather report stating that the first tropical storm of the season had formed west of Barbados. It was still in its early stages with seventy-five-mile-an-hour winds and moving west-northwest at seventeen miles per hour. Fortunately, the *Suzy Wong* saw no sign of the storm in its current location. There were light winds from the east all day.

While the crew was on the lookout for the hurricane, a large fish, estimated at six to eight feet, struck their jury-rigged fishing line. From a distance of twenty yards, the crew saw the fish leap into the air with a mighty effort and head straight down into the ocean depths, reeling out all of the 250-pound test line and snapping it. They weren't fish experts by any means, but George swore it was a swordfish.

By mid-afternoon the boat entered the waters of the Bahamas, passing San Salvador Island where Christopher Columbus first landed in North America. His voyage had taken him on a more northerly course, putting him in the doldrums. The *Suzy Wong*, on the other hand, had followed the easterly trade winds south across the Atlantic. And, of course, the *Suzy* crew had the advantage of maps, charts, and hindsight. Nonetheless, these four sailors now had a first-hand understanding of what a monumental undertaking it was to sail across the Atlantic. As they passed the island, they enjoyed a moment of camaraderie and new-found respect for those long-passed adventurers of 1492.

The next day, July 21, the crew turned on the radio and heard a news account of Gus Grissom's flight into space. As one of seven members of the Mercury space program, he made a fifteen-minute suborbital flight into space aboard the *Liberty Bell 7* capsule that day. After a purposeful splashdown into the Atlantic, explosive bolts holding the emergency exit hatch blew without warning and water filled the capsule, forcing Grissom into the ocean. The Coast Guard rescued him by helicopter, but the capsule sank.

By the crew's calculations, Gus Grissom must have touched down within fifty miles of the *Suzy Wong*'s location. They were, however, unable to see any of the recovery ships or the capsule's re-entry trail. They thought it would have been great if Grissom had landed close to them; they could have pulled him aboard and taken him home to a hero's welcome—his and theirs.

The distance from St. Thomas to Nassau in the Bahamas is 770 nautical miles, which the *Suzy Wong* sailed in just under a week. The crew sighted Eleuthera Island, rounded its northern tip, and spotted the Egg Island lighthouse. At 2030h a celestial fix showed their location in safe water, just eight miles north-northwest of Man Island.

In the hours just after dawn on the morning of July 22, 1961, they entered Nassau Harbor, Bahamas. Thirty minutes later the *Suzy Wong* ran aground on a sandbar just west of Yacht Haven. It was no big deal to the guys. They threw out two anchors and waited for the tide to float the boat free. After a short delay of two-and-a-half hours, the sailors were able to raise the anchors and head into port.

They stayed in Nassau for four days during which Walt's mother joined her son and his sailing companions. She would sail with them on the very last leg of their voyage to the United States.

CHAPTER 47

THE LAST LEG OF THE VOYAGE

At 0720h on July 26, 1961, George, Steve, Walt, Paul, and Gou embarked on the last sail of their seventeen-month, 26,000-mile voyage from Hong Kong to Florida. With Walt's mother, Constance, along for the ride, they departed Yacht Haven in Nassau, heading due west on a course for the US mainland. Light easterly winds filled the sails and the *Suzy Wong* made good time.

The guys thought Walt's mother was one of the most delightful guests they ever had on board. She was cheerful, friendly, helpful, and never once gave advice or suggested a better way of doing things. This was a surprise because there were still more than a few things that could have used improvement, and she certainly must have had suggestions in mind.

A day out of Nassau, the crew considered taking a swim in the ocean. Often during the voyage they would face the boat into the wind and post a person on deck with a Winchester 30/30. The man on deck would watch for sharks and be available to handle the boat in the event it started sailing away. Another guy would go into the water wearing goggles to look out for sharks that might attack from underneath. Meanwhile the remaining crew would dive in and enjoy a swim. From the water, they'd call to Gou to join them and, sure enough, he would do his best dive and paddle around with them in the ocean.

Gou was generally the last to come aboard, as he had to be lifted back onto deck—all wet and shaking. Gou weighed fifty pounds to start with and probably 10 pounds more when soaking wet. It took a strong crewman to grab him by the neck and backside and lift him out of the water.

On this particular day prior to jumping into the sea, Paul thought he might do some fishing to see what he could catch for dinner. Lacking any lures or bait, he put a bright piece of red nylon on the hook and cast out his line. Almost immediately he got a heavy tug indicating he had hooked something big. He tugged, twisted, and reeled the line in, only to have it spin out again. He could see he was going to have a fight on his hands. Sweat began pouring down his face. George went for his Winchester gun because he knew the landing net wouldn't hold this fish. He offered to trade places with Paul to allow him a rest, but Paul said, "No, this one is mine!"

Paul wrestled with his catch for nearly an hour before the line suddenly went slack. The fight was gone, but something was still there. And whatever it was, it was extremely heavy. As it rose closer to the surface, Paul saw that it was a large fish followed by a…"Shark!" he yelled. George immediately pumped several rounds at the shark, which finally let go of the fish and dove out of sight.

Paul had caught what would have been at least a fifty-pound tuna if the shark hadn't eaten half of it away. The fish was about the diameter of Paul's thigh, which was considerable since Paul was a big guy. Not wanting to miss a memory, Steve recorded the event with his movie camera, showing the upper half of the tuna dangling from the line with only jagged tooth marks where the tail had once been. That evening the four men, Walt's mother, and Gou enjoyed eighteen pounds of fresh tuna!

During the entire voyage the crew never had much use for the odd assortment of weapons they had worked so hard to bring aboard before departing Hong Kong. All they ever shot was a lone shark, some big fish, and sea snakes. George, a crack shot, handled them all.

At 2115h that same day, the log noted, "Sighted Great Isaac Light. Moon is full and the wind has died." The most prominent feature of this small island was its 150-foot tall lighthouse, which was erected in 1859. Local lore told of a shipwreck near the island in the late nineteenth century during which an infant was lost. The child's distraught mother, known as the Grey Lady, was said to haunt the island through all eternity, wailing in sorrow with every full moon. During the crew's full moon, however, the Grey Lady was disappointingly silent and any ghostly infants remained in their unearthly slumber.

On the last day before landing in Florida, the four guys sorted through their many possessions to decide what they needed to get rid of before going through US customs. They had medical supplies in case someone needed stitches or an emergency appendectomy. They had morphine, medical books, a scalpel, a hemostat, and various other things they had picked up in Hong Kong. They didn't want to take any of these somewhat illicit items through customs because of the hassle and potential red tape. After the scrutiny, the sailors filed their unnecessary supplies and questionable contraband at the bottom of the Atlantic Ocean for safekeeping.

Coming to the end of their journey, the crew had to handle one final bit of painful business—they had to decide what to do with Gou. All four men had fallen deeply in love with their beautiful white Chinese Chow and they all wanted him. Since Walt's mother was aboard and considered a disinterested fifth party, she conducted a raffle to determine who would get to take the dog home. The stakes were high. Walt's mother held out her hand and the four guys drew straws. As it turned out, Paul won the drawing and would be Gou's master upon the completion of their voyage.

The *Suzy Wong* passed through the Lake Worth inlet into Palm Beach Harbor on July 28 at 1400h. The boat was flying the usual yellow quarantine flag signaling that the crew hadn't yet passed through customs or immigration. Walt's dad had driven down from his home in Chattanooga to pick up Constance and he met the boat at the pier. Unfortunately, US Customs and Immigration wouldn't permit anyone to leave the boat, as the crew hadn't paid the required deposit money for import duties and taxes. This was completely unexpected.

Not knowing what to do next, Steve called his dad, who found a solution to this dilemma with the help of a Miami customs broker, Captain Lemay. After all, the crew was importing a Chinese-built boat into the United States; duties and taxes were due. The funny thing was that Immigration had cleared Gou, the dog, back in the Virgin Islands, but not the men. Technically, Gou could have sauntered off to enjoy Palm Beach high society while the guys waited for clearance, confined to the boat and the pier.

Captain Lemay directed the sailors to leave West Palm Beach immediately and sail to Miami. Walt's dad got on the road and headed south to meet them. The crew had only one more day of sailing. As they backed the boat out of her berth, the tide caught *Suzy* and drove her into two pilings, causing some slight damage. Undeterred, they sailed down the east coast of Florida past the towns of Lake Worth, Boca Raton, Ft. Lauderdale, and Hollywood before reaching their final destination.

At 1530h on July 30, 1961, the long, successful journey came to an end. The *Suzy* crew were welcomed into the United States at City Yacht Basin, Miami. Needless to say, the men were pleased to be home, having completed this extraordinary voyage of some 26,000 miles and seventeen months at sea. They had come a long way, both in distance and in spirit.

But the crew had no time to celebrate; they still had a lot of work to do. They said goodbye to Walt's parents, who drove home to Tennessee. Next, they had to focus their attention on all the business at hand. They needed to take out a loan on the boat to cover expenses for the time it would take to refurbish the *Suzy Wong* and put her on the market. The loan would also be used to pay off the debt they still owed to American Marine Limited for the boat's construction. Finally, they needed to find a place to dry dock *Suzy* for the refurbishing. After asking around for recommendations, the crew agreed to motor her up the Miami River to the Jones Boat Yard.

There, they began their final maintenance work. They painted the *Suzy Wong* from top to bottom and cleaned her cabin until it practically glistened like new. They gave an extra shine to the beautifully carved teakwood plaque that had been crafted in Hong Kong and installed on the forward bulkhead of the boat. It listed the names, in Chinese characters, of all the workers who had built the boat, and it was dedicated to Tin Hau, Chinese goddess of the sea. Its purpose had been to bring the Americans good luck on their voyage. Indeed, Tin Hau had served them well.

Talisman for safe passage, Tin Hau, Chinese goddess of the sea

Part of the process of readying the *Suzy Wong* for sale was to examine and repair all of her mechanical components. The crew's big equipment splurge had been a depth sounder, which they thought necessary for fathom navigation and shallow-water piloting. This electronic wonder functioned for less than a week before dying. At their very first port of call in the Philippines, George and Walt had removed it and sent it for repair via military postal service back to Seattle's manufacturer, Ross Labs. It was returned to the *Suzy Wong* almost a year later when they were in Spain, and George and Walt reinstalled it. Once again it failed to function, so it was stowed away and forgotten.

The Jones Boat Yard was really the first place where Walt got a chance to examine the mostly unused depth sounder. In doing so, he discovered the reason for its malfunction. Evidently the manufacturer had packed the unit in popcorn for safe shipping and a single kernel of popcorn had gotten jammed into the rotating depth indicator. Extracting the kernel was all that was needed for it to work like new.

Meanwhile, they decided that each crew member should have a memento. Walt got the logbook because he had done such a great job of keeping the records during the voyage. A silver plaque engraved with the crew's names went to George. Paul was always involved with their busy social calendar and the guest book, so he took those. Steve's souvenir was the set of signal flags first used at the boat's launching in Junk Bay.

Finally, each sailor signed his name to the last page of the ship's log and the guest book. Paul added Gou's name and paw print as well, which was only fitting, as the dog had been with them every step of the way.

The voyage of the *Suzy Wong* was now officially over!

CHAPTER 48

SAYING GOODBYE

Steve was in charge of selling the boat. In a letter to his parents dated August 2, 1961, he wrote:

> The brokers think this is a great boat. One of the best they have seen out of the Orient. We will make our decision soon as to which broker will handle the sale. Then we can float a loan on the boat to get us through…. There shouldn't be any trouble getting the loan.

In truth the crew had difficulty finding someone to loan them money. After many turndowns, Walt and George found a banker who was also a sailor and therefore could discern that *Suzy* would be well protected at the Jones Boat Yard and that she was certainly worth much more than the $9,000 loan request. This banker worked out a six-month deal for the requested amount.

The crew faced yet another snafu in registering the boat. The law for bringing in a foreign-made boat allowed six months after completion of its construction to apply for and finalize registration. The four men had been underway for seventeen months and there was no category for that on the application. A bit of pleading and a case of whiskey solved that dilemma. Then they had to determine the boat's value for tax purposes. The *Suzy Wong* was, after all, a used boat and thus its import valuation needed to take that into consideration.

On August 17 Steve wrote his parents again:

> Work on *Suzy* is nearly complete. The first of next week should see her finished…. To date we have paid the duty, had the boat measured for registration and documentation, arranged for insurance, and are

in the process of negotiating a loan. In other words, I should be able to start north by the end of next week. Paul and Gou will be with me.

As soon as the crew received their $9,000 six-month loan, they paid off the expenses accrued during refurbishment and they repaid Bob Newton of American Marine Limited. The boatyard allowed the four men to do their own work on *Suzy*, which saved them a lot of money. They rented a small motel room near the boatyard so they wouldn't have to commute far to work.

Throughout their voyage, the crew had faced weather that was extremely hot, muggy, and dusty. They had had to contend with bugs, rats, snakes, unwashed natives with guns, and non-potable water. And yet, in all their travels, they never experienced conditions like they found in Miami. It felt like a sauna from which they couldn't escape. Within minutes after getting dressed each day, their clothes were drenched in sweat. The time spent in Miami felt interminable. They were ready to be done.

After spending seventeen months together in cramped quarters and depending on each other for their very lives, the crew bid farewell to one another with mixed feelings. They were sad to bring this grand adventure to a close, but also eager to move on and start the next chapter of their lives.

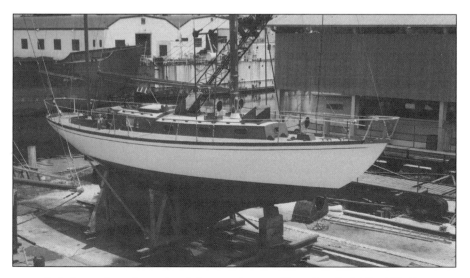

Lady *Suzy*—dressed up and ready for new adventures! Jones Boat Yard, Miami, Florida

George bought a rusty late-1940s DeSoto for fifty bucks and drove Walt to his home in Chattanooga, Tennessee. He continued on to northern New York to visit his mother and turned the DeSoto over to his sister. Then he rejoined Walt in New York City and the two of them drove Walt's roadster to Seattle, where they both took up residence.

Steve bought a 1950 Chrysler in pretty good condition for ninety-five dollars. He, Paul, and Gou drove all the way to Steve's parents' home in South Salem, New York, arriving on August 28 after several long, hot days of driving.

By the completion of the voyage, the four men had managed to get the name *Suzy Wong* mentioned in twenty-four newspapers in various ports around the world. Some were written in Chinese and some in Arabic, but they all clearly read "*Suzie Wong*" or "*Suzy Wong*." The publicity department of Paramount Pictures paid the crew $1,200 at the end of the trip—fifty dollars for each mention, as promised.

It was another five months before the *Suzy Wong* was sold, just one week before the six-month, $9,000 loan came due. The boat sold for $32,000. After paying for the commission on the sale, they had $30,000 to divide up in proportion to their ownership interests as originally agreed upon. In total, the four Americans came out about even. They had hoped for a financial killing, but that didn't happen. What they walked away with was a return of their invested capital and, of course, a thrilling adventure. Their seemingly endless good luck and constant penny-pinching had paid off.

The *Suzy Wong* had been bought by well-known author and conservative political commentator, William F. Buckley.

Chapter 49

Paul

Paul became close with Mary through their correspondence and brief encounters during his seventeen months at sea. In fact, they had fallen in love and planned to marry in Madrid. Since he couldn't take Gou overseas, Steve's parents offered to care for Gou until Paul returned from Spain and could integrate the dog into his newly married life.

But first he had to attend to some personal business. Paul had not been home to California in almost two years and had put many matters on hold, such as his house in Palo Alto. He also wanted to visit his many friends and relatives. He found extremely inexpensive charter flights from the East Coast to San Francisco. The airlines had begun using jet planes for their flights, but they were more expensive so he chose to travel by a propeller plane. He was on the West Coast for three weeks putting his personal life in order. Then he returned to Spain, flying from San Francisco to New York, then to Scotland, and on to Madrid—all on prop engine aircraft, and all at low cost.

Although finding a job was foremost on his mind, Paul and Mary decided it would be best for her to complete her State Department contract in Madrid, which would end in another year. From a financial standpoint, this plan was essential. It was the only way to have her car and household goods shipped back to the States at government expense. They decided to take one life-changing step at a time, so marriage was put first and Paul's career would have to wait until later.

Paul and Mary took their vows on December 2, 1961, at the British Embassy Anglican Church of Saint George in Madrid, Spain. But this was actually their second ceremony. At the time, Spain didn't allow a mixed marriage between a Catholic and a non-Catholic, so they tied the knot four days earlier in Gibraltar—the closest place to Madrid where they could legally get married.

Paul's search for employment in Spain produced nothing he felt would be suitable. After having championed such an extraordinary adventure for the past two years, an ordinary desk job or a nine-to-five position with a predictable routine held no appeal. His sense of adventure had been helplessly unleashed while sampling so many of the great feasts the world had to offer. Paul believed there was more awaiting him and he didn't want to make a permanent choice now. Instead, he found a temporary job that seemed perfect for him. He had always been an avid card player, being particularly successful at bridge. So Paul began his married life as the bridge instructor at the Torrejon Airbase Officers' Wives Club. He was paid by the lesson in cash.

At the end of Mary's contract, the newlyweds set sail (on an ocean liner this time) for the United States' eastern seaboard. They arrived with their Spanish car, a Simca, which they drove across the country to California. The trip was uneventful until they crossed the California line, where a highway patrolman pulled them over. Their traffic offense was having amber headlights—required in Spain, but not acceptable in California. They were given a traffic ticket as a belated wedding present.

In southern California the newlyweds visited Mary's mother and brother and then drove north to Palo Alto to settle into Paul's house. Paul had spent a year considering his next professional move and decided he wanted to try his hand in the travel business. In one form or another, he wanted to continue the personal journey he had begun two years earlier—traveling the world and meeting new people. And he wanted to continue to be his own boss. Paul knew he could never go back to a large organization like Standard Oil or the Post Office.

He worked for a construction company by day and pursued his travel business at night, planning tours and devising the techniques for selling them. Working with a local fashion editor, his first tour featured art and fashion, taking women living in the Palo Alto area to visit the great fashion houses in Madrid, Rome, Florence, and Paris.

Soon he bought a nearly defunct travel company that he and Mary built into one of the largest agencies in northern California. They ran their

Adventure Travel Service for two decades. One of his signature activities was organizing Stanford University football tours.

Paul and Mary had two sons, Tony and John, who in turn gave them two granddaughters, Katie and Elizabeth.

Travel had brought Mary and Paul together and their family held them together, but their professional paths ultimately led them in different directions. They were divorced in 1990 and continued to head separate travel companies in Palo Alto, remaining close friends until Mary's death from cancer in 2009.

Years after the voyage of *Suzy Wong*, Paul was able to return to Hong Kong. He visited many of his old haunts, including Rikki's, where his Suzy Wong Salad was still on the menu.

CHAPTER 50

WALTER

Upon completion of their grand adventure and after some time visiting family and friends, Walt and George decided to become business partners, so they met in New York and drove west to Seattle, Washington, seeking their next adventure.

In the summer of 1963, during his required annual active duty with the US Navy, Walt met Yvonne Goldman on a blind date in San Francisco. They were married on December 28, 1963, in San Francisco, and Yvonne gave birth to their twin sons the following Thanksgiving. Walt served the remaining years of his Naval Reserve duty flying a Douglas Skyraider dive-bomber based at the naval air station in Seattle. He retired from the military in the late 1970s after attaining the rank of commander.

Soon after arriving in Seattle, Walt landed a position with Harstad Associates, a consulting engineering firm specializing in major real estate property development. After a couple of years of learning the business and obtaining his professional engineer's license, Walt became project engineer for the master development plan of Southampton, a proposed new city surrounding the small town of Benicia, California. Walt then moved on to other opportunities before this project came to fruition. Southampton was, in later years, developed primarily according to Walt's plan—right down to the English street names taken late one night by George and Walt from an English railway travel book.

Eventually Walt and George pooled resources to purchase the Saint Regis Hotel in downtown Seattle, a 133-room residential building that was in extremely poor condition after the 1962 Seattle World's Fair. This joint business venture had actually been the motivation for Walt to enter the engineering field and obtain his license.

The first few years of running the hotel was a struggle due to a major earthquake, little or no funding, and their lack of experience at hotel management. The venture, however, provided them with valuable real-life experiences in dealing with all levels of humanity around the clock. Eventually, the hotel, which included a restaurant and a somewhat notorious nightclub, turned a profit and became a launching pad for other ventures in real estate development.

The two men ended their partnership in early 1990 after selling the hotel to the City of Seattle for use as a rehabilitation center for alcoholics. Walt returned to aviation as an avocation, buying an interest in a Christen Eagle sports biplane and entering the world of competitive aerobatics. He also partnered with several senior Boeing engineers and built a Lancair IV-P aircraft. This was a state-of-the-art, high-performance aircraft, constructed of carbon fiber by some of the same people who designed the Boeing 787 now in commercial service. It was another learning experience for Walt. Unfortunately, the aircraft was destroyed in a serious accident that badly injured one of his partners. Walt continued to fly for many years, but he gave up the sport of competitive aerobatics.

Walt and Yvonne have lived in the same home overlooking Lake Washington in Seattle for more than forty years. Their sons, David and Lee, presently live near each other in the Marina District of San Francisco. Both are married and have given Walt and Yvonne grandchildren.

Chapter 51

George

George left Miami at the end of the *Suzy Wong* voyage and drove with Walt to Seattle, Washington, where he now resides. George shared ownership of a small hotel with Walt for a number of years, but that was not to be his long-term legacy. After sailing halfway around the world, he wanted another *Suzy Wong* in his life. Of all the crew members, George became the most committed, lifelong sailor.

George built a boat that would indulge his whims and fantasies, enable him to go sailing again, and even become his home when he eventually retired. He knew it would be prudent to put his time and effort into a craft that was large enough to charter, and thus pay expenses. It took him ten years to accomplish this dream. The result was a sixty-five-foot schooner that he named the *Mallory Todd* after a legendary sea captain from Scotland. George had the boat exquisitely finished with hand-rubbed mahogany, antique stained glass, and etched brass and artifacts from his world cruise. The boat's main saloon and captain's cabin also featured porcelain fireplaces designed in the gracious style of a bygone era.

The dock used by the *Mallory Todd* was within sight of the Seattle Cancer Care Alliance. When some of the younger patients were well enough to go outside, they started hanging around his dock in the summertime. Kids being pretty hard to turn down, George began inviting them and their parents aboard. He would take them for a sail around the lake, and the kids just loved it. Soon George was hooked, and his plans for the future changed dramatically.

George became dedicated to bringing the peace and solace he felt upon the water into the lives of others. He created the Sailing Heritage Society, a nonprofit organization to help thousands of children and families learn about the sea and sailing. "Sailors Helping Kids" was the call to action behind his highly effective community service program.

George continued taking the *Mallory Todd* out to the San Juan Islands or into Puget Sound on private charters, which helped to fund his nonprofit organization. What started as just a few of those special trips per year eventually totaled more than two hundred over the course of a decade. The Sailing Heritage Society expanded its outreach to include young stroke victims, families dealing with domestic abuse, and other such groups.

Some may think sailing to be a passive experience for the passenger, but George felt otherwise. He knew that just being on board a ship did people a lot of good. This kind of recreational therapy could go a long way to help the healing process—not just for a person's body, but for his mind and spirit as well. When passengers sailed on the *Mallory Todd* with George at the helm, they weren't thinking about their pain or discomfort or sadness. They were just getting out in the sun and fresh air, enjoying the experience of being on the water, and having fun.

George always wished more people, wherever they lived, would take the initiative to do the same thing. He knew there were thousands of boats sitting idle in harbors or tied up to docks all across the country, hardly ever going out on the water. George's long-term goal was to put together a consortium of boat owners, captains, crew, and volunteers to spread this kind of experience to other cities.

George continues to sail his boat on Seattle's Puget Sound and Lake Washington for both business and pleasure. It was George's participation in the *Suzy Wong* voyage that inspired him to chart a meaningful and inspiring journey for the rest of his life.

Chapter 52

Steve

A few days after Steve's return home to South Salem, New York, his parents threw a gala welcome-home party on their lawn. An enormous tent sheltered hundreds of celebrating relatives, neighbors, and friends. One of the invited neighbors was Henry A. Wallace, Secretary of Agriculture in the cabinet of President Franklin D. Roosevelt from 1933 to 1940 and Roosevelt's vice president from 1940 to 1945.

Steve had kept up a lively exchange of letters and visits with Pat from the moment they met in Barbados. She lived in Chicago and Steve wanted nothing more than to be with her. So he left New York for the Midwest and took a position as a supervisory trainee with the Continental Can Company in Chicago. Steve and Pat were married in her hometown, Louisville, Kentucky, on September 29, 1962. Theirs was another beautiful *Suzy Wong*–inspired wedding. Their daughter, Deborah, was born in 1965 and their son, Charles, followed in 1969.

Coincidentally, Steve's daughter Deborah had a chance meeting with Paul's son Tony when they both worked for Motorola in Beijing, China. They became good friends.

Pat worked for the Council of State Governments, a job she enjoyed very much. Her boss eventually introduced her to the Bahá'í teachings, which she shared with Steve. They were intrigued with this spiritual path and spent a year studying everything they could about the new world religion. Steve and Pat became Bahá'ís at the end of 1963.

Steve decided Continental Can was not where he wanted to spend the rest of his working days, nor was he doing what he really wanted to do. He began work on his MBA at the University of Chicago and completed his degree in finance in 1964. After graduate school, Steve worked for the Trane (air-conditioning) Company for five years in Washington, D.C., and then for the Chemical Bank for another five years in New York City. The long commute into the city each day didn't suit him, so he looked elsewhere for a more personally fulfilling work situation. He accepted a position as the Chief Financial Officer at the Bahá'í National Center in Wilmette, Illinois, spending the next seventeen years managing the Treasurer's Office, where his skills and experience with accounting, budgeting, economic analysis, and travel were perfectly matched.

Steve's experience sailing the *Suzy Wong* had a profound influence on his life. Not only did he and Pat find each other at the journey's end, but it also inspired his humanitarian service for the next four decades. After his tenure at the Bahá'í National Center, he became a consultant for the World Bank, the United Nations (UNDP), USAID, and the Experiment for International Living—all in Africa. Following that, he and Pat lived and taught at the University of Nanjing in China for five years. They immersed themselves in the cultures and societies of foreign lands and places. Unfortunately, after 43 years of married life, Pat passed away in 2007 from a rare form of blood cancer.

Steve is now happily married to Ruth Skomurski, an old friend from a neighboring city. Ruth spent most of her life teaching music to children in the schools and homes of Highland Park, Illinois, and is an accomplished pianist and musician. Like Steve, Ruth is a Bahá'í, but hardly the traveler that Steve is. At the time of their marriage, Ruth didn't even have a passport. But Steve took care of that—he whisked her off to Italy for a biking-holiday honeymoon and then to Haifa, Israel, for a Bahá'í mini-pilgrimage. She quickly learned the joys of international travel. Steve and Ruth live in Deerfield, Illinois.

CHAPTER 53

GOU

Gou may have been a dog, but he was a cherished member of the *Suzy Wong* crew. He was a friend to each man, a swimming partner in mid-ocean, a sweet-tempered animal, and always a companion to whomever was on the helm at any given moment. Gou was such an extraordinary, well-behaved mascot that people along the way fell in love with him and often wanted to buy him. The crew always refused such offers.

From the start, people with sailing experience advised the young crew against taking the dog on the voyage. They warned of difficulties taking care of his needs and even the potential danger to his safety during storms or in challenging situations. But looking back from a distance of many years, the crew unanimously agreed that including Gou was one of their best decisions.

Each of the *Suzy*'s crewmen wanted to keep Gou after the voyage, but none of them were really in a position to take him. They weren't yet settled in a place where a dog could live comfortably and run freely. Even Paul, who won Gou in the drawing, wasn't prepared to take Gou, as he would be traveling overseas to get married. Alas, Gou was left with Steve's parents, Robert and Laura Jackson.

Gou settled quickly into life with the Jacksons in rural South Salem. He was no longer confined to just a few square feet of deck space. Now he had miles of farmland and fields to roam and explore. From the Jacksons' home, the neighboring properties extended endlessly in all directions. Just as he had done in the Canary Islands (where he disappeared for several days), it was not uncommon for Gou to take off running. Neighbors would call the Jacksons to inform them that their dog was five or six miles from home. Robert and Laura never worried because Gou always managed to find his way back home in time for supper.

The dog's day-to-day routine had changed drastically as well. Instead of having four guys pulling his tail and roughhousing with him each day, he spent much of his time by Laura's side. He accompanied her to bridge club luncheons and beauty parlor visits that took up large blocks of time each day. The world-traveled Gou had become an ordinary citizen of South Salem, New York, accepted wherever he went.

Sadly, Paul's reunion with Gou would never happen. Having started the voyage as a puppy and grown up on the boat, Gou knew the sea and the sailboat well, but he wasn't familiar with the dangers on land. It was his penchant for running that eventually got him into trouble. Just a year after the voyage ended, Gou darted onto a winding country road and was struck by an oncoming automobile. Befitting his high place of honor as beloved pet and mascot, Gou was buried on the grounds of the property that had become his first and only home on land.

CHAPTER 54

SUZY SAILS ON

In 1962, the *Suzy Wong* was sold to a new owner named William F. Buckley. The *Suzy Wong* became part of Buckley's lifelong obsession with boats and sailing. He acquired his first sailboat, which he named *Sweet Isolation*, when he was just a teenager. He followed that with a larger vessel called the *Panic*, which he bought with his brother in 1954. A hurricane destroyed the *Panic* in 1961, uprooting it from its mooring and smashing it onto the rocks of a nearby breakwater in the Stamford, Connecticut, Yacht Club Harbor.

In his 2004 sailing memoir, *Aweigh*, Buckley wrote about his acquisition of the *Suzy Wong*. A passage in the book reads:

> Boat owners tend to upgrade, and I now had the insurance money. I very quickly bought, sight unseen, a forty-one foot Sparkman & Stephens yawl of illustrious design (Nevins 40) from its four owners in Miami. It was offered with a piquant story. The sailors had served together in the Army in Japan and, aged twenty to twenty-two, had dreamed of owning a sailboat and taking it around the world.

Buckley got some of the facts wrong about the *Suzy Wong* crew. They were indeed former servicemen, but only George and Steve served together and that was in the Philippines, not Japan. Their ages were also wrong—the youngest member was Steve, who was twenty-six at the time the voyage started, while Paul was the oldest at thirty-three.

Buckley's account continues:

> They could put together only enough money to buy the bare boat and engine from the American boat company in Hong Kong. It

was all teak—teakwood was cheap in that part of the world.... They sanded and painted the hull, mounted the rigging, installed the plumbing and electrical systems, and finished the deck. Two months later the boat was ready, and they set out, westward, for Miami, arriving months later, flat broke and happy. They calculated that they had spent a dollar and seventy-five cents per person per day....I paid them $30,000 for the *Suzy Wong*, and sailed her for sixteen years, some weekdays, most summer weekends, here and there cruising on blue water, running two races to Bermuda and one to Halifax.

Buckley's son, Christopher T. Buckley, wrote about his sailing experiences with his father in his own book, *My Old Man and the Sea*.

Christopher described the *Suzy Wong* as,

...a sweet, 41-foot Sparkman & Stephens yawl, Hong Kong-built. She was a real honey, all teak and mahogany and with carved Buddhas. Every summer we would cruise the waters of Maine aboard *Suzy*. Sailing in Maine was always an adventure. The water is scrotum-tighteningly cold, the currents swift, the tidal drop pronounced, and the bottom unforgivingly rocky.

He recounts the happy times on board the *Suzy Wong* and the unforgettable sailing lessons taught him by his father on her deck.

Steve kept in touch with William Buckley for many years. He had gotten to know Buckley, who asked Steve to captain the *Suzy* after the boat suffered rigging problems and had to pull out of the Annapolis-Newport race one year. Buckley had to be elsewhere in the world and needed a skipper to sail from Norfolk, Virginia, to New York City. Steve got to learn a lot from Buckley's crew about their sailing adventures and misadventures.

In 1978 William Buckley decided to upgrade once again when he acquired a sixty-foot schooner he named the *Cyrano*. He sold the *Suzy Wong* to Harvard

Business School graduate and business consultant, Steve Dichter, who lived in Boston and had seen an ad for *Suzy*. Dichter traveled to Stamford, Connecticut, to meet with Buckley and see the boat. Buckley mentioned its maiden voyage from Hong Kong to Miami in 1960–1961, but Dichter learned nothing else about the boat or its original owners.

Dichter had had wooden boats all his life. At one time he had converted a twenty-four-foot lifeboat and sailed it from Philadelphia to the Bahamas. One look at the *Suzy Wong* and he wanted her. Dichter and his girlfriend, Cheri Marshall, signed the sales contract with Buckley on July 2, 1981, taking possession of the boat in August of that year. Years later, the *New York Times Magazine* quoted Buckley's wife, Pat, about the sale of the boat:

> *Suzy Wong*, his [Bill's] teak yawl, was bought by a charming but obviously seriously demented young couple whose dream in life was to own and maintain a wooden boat. In fact, they now spend every free hour of what they consider an idyllic existence scraping and painting *Suzy*—and whatever else one does to an all-wood craft.

After a few months of refurbishment, the couple anchored the boat in the Dotson Boatyard of Stonington, Connecticut, and used it for coastal cruising. People were always drawn to the boat wherever Dichter anchored or docked, always commenting on the boat's inherent grace and beauty.

Once while docked in Camden, Maine, a drunken sailor staggered up to Dichter and said he knew of the boat. Dichter didn't think much of this since William F. Buckley had written extensively about the boat, so everyone knew of the *Suzy Wong*. Then the sailor said, "Hong Kong. 1960. I was there."

It turned out that this unidentified man had been one of the hundreds of people who had clambered over the *Suzy Wong* at the launching celebration just before its four original owners embarked on their sailing adventure. To prove his claim, the drunken sailor pointed out several features of the boat that even Dichter hadn't noticed before that very moment. Dichter later regretted that he didn't think to ask for the man's name and record it in his log.

In 1984, Dichter was living in New York City and had the *Suzy Wong* docked in City Island, New York. The *New York Times* was looking for photographs to use in their Memorial Day summer season feature and a photographer asked if he could take a few shots of the boat. Dichter didn't believe the guy was really with the *New York Times* until he was walking out of his apartment the next day, on May 23, 1984, and the doorman of his building pointed out that the *Suzy Wong* was prominently displayed on the front page.

It was that newspaper photo that came to the attention of one of the original co-owners, Steve Jackson, who then used the telephone book and made several calls to locate Dichter. When the two men met, Steve told Ditcher a brief history of the *Suzy Wong*.

In the spring of 1982, Walt flew east with his twin sons to tour Washington, D.C., New York, and Boston as part of his sons' high school senior program. Walt landed his twin-engine plane initially at the Westchester County Airport, a small private field near White Plains, NY. They called William Buckley to see if they could visit the *Suzy Wong*. Mr. Buckley's administrative assistant said the boat had been sold to Steve Dichter and gave his number in Boston. Dichter was kind enough to meet Walt and sons at the South Boston Marina where *Suzy* was docked. It was most moving for Walt to show his sons the vessel upon which he had taken his greatest adventure. The boat was a bit worn, but still in good shape. Steve Dichter knew very little of the history of the voyage so Walt took the opportunity to fill him in and spend a couple of hours on board the boat. Walt has stayed in touch with Dichter over the years, but never again has he seen *Suzy*.

In September 1985, Hurricane Gloria roared up the East Coast where the *Suzy Wong* was moored in Stonington, Connecticut. The winds knocked her off her mooring and threw the boat fifty yards inland into someone's backyard. Miraculously, the boat landed in a sandy spot so the damage was mostly cosmetic. She was back sailing and looking as good as ever the following summer.

Dichter was married on Block Island, Rhode Island, and even sailed some of his wedding guests to the ceremony on the *Suzy Wong*. After owning the boat for nearly a decade, Dichter decided he didn't have time in his busy life for sailing. He sold the boat in 1990 to a man from Manahawkin, New Jersey.

CHAPTER 55

SUZY REBORN

The history of the *Suzy Wong* gets cloudy after its 1990 purchase by a New Jersey man. At some point in the late 1990s, a drug smuggler was in possession of the boat and ran it aground in New Jersey's Barnegut Bay while running from the Coast Guard with a full load of drugs aboard. The DEA seized the *Suzy Wong* and put the boat up for auction, at which point a man named Frank Fontecone bought it thinking he could just put a coat of paint on it and go sailing around the world. When he found out it wasn't as simple a proposition as that, the *Suzy Wong* was put up for sale yet again.

Dan Beltram, owner of a quality chefs' knife company, had loved boats all his life. He had built a number of small wooden boats over the years and decided it was time to do something more adventurous. He and his wife, Maureen, set out to find a boat that he could restore, but they had certain parameters. The first was the boat's location—it had to be on the eastern seaboard so they wouldn't have to sail it through the Panama Canal or truck it across the United States to get it home. Secondly, they had three boat designers in mind—their first preference was a Sparkman & Stephens boat. Finally, they wanted a boat with a pedigree and a history if they were going to spend the money, time, and effort to restore it.

Dan and Maureen followed many leads and looked at countless boats. Some of the boats were only days away from being chain-sawed for scrap. Some were worth looking at, but the price was too high. With every boat they considered, from the top of Maine to the tip of Florida, Maureen's first comment was, "This is ridiculous." They were all wrecks.

But in 2002 the couple's son-in-law, Emil, and daughter, Laura, had gone to a boat show and were flipping through a listing of boats for sale when they saw the *Suzy Wong*. Emil suggested that Laura call her parents to tell them about the boat. After doing so, Laura called the boat broker to try and arrange a viewing. Meanwhile, her father followed her tip and called the boat broker at almost the exact same time. The broker said he had a woman on the other line inquiring about the same boat, and Dan yelled to his wife, "Hey, Maureen, someone's trying to take my boat." Dan couldn't have known that he almost got into a bidding war with his own daughter.

Dan and Maureen went to Forked River, New Jersey, to look at the *Suzy Wong*. She was in bad shape, with ugly green paint chipping off her sides. But Dan had hired a boat surveyor who gave *Suzy* a favorable report, saying she was worth restoring. Also, this was the only boat the Beltrams looked at where Maureen didn't say, "This is ridiculous." So Dan knew the *Suzy Wong* was a keeper. He bought the boat in the fall of 2002.

A sorrowful sight, aging *Suzy* awaits her savior; Tall Oaks Marina, Forked River, New Jersey

His next challenge was finding a place to work on *Suzy* because a lot of boat yards simply didn't want to take on a wooden boat. Many restoration projects on these older sailing vessels would begin, only to be later abandoned, leaving the boatyard with a wooden boat that no one else wanted. After looking all around, Dan finally found a storage yard in Hamburg, New Jersey, that would accept the boat the following May. In the meantime, Beltram built a wooden structure with a corrugated roof on the site where he would begin the restoration work on *Suzy*.

In May of 2003 Beltram trucked the *Suzy Wong* up to the Hamburg storage yard. He and son-in-law, Emil, set forth three phases for the project: demolition, valuation, and restoration. The demolition process took the better part of a year, during which time they took much of the boat apart piece by piece. They had to look at each board to decide if it could be reused or if it needed to be discarded and replaced. Part of this chore was deciding just how much of the boat to take apart.

New owner, Dan Beltram, with helpers, Ray Ambrosi and Emil Stoessel; Hamburg, New Jersey

Every time they took something apart, they found more rot and something else that needed to be fixed. It was clear to Beltram that a couple of the previous owners had not done sufficient maintenance on her. They made the decision to take *Suzy* completely apart and refasten all of her frames and plankings.

The original Burmese teak on the planking was ninety percent salvageable, but the sternpost was worm-eaten and had to be replaced. They had to install a brand new forepeak and bow stem and repair the damage done to the hull from the drug smugglers having run it aground.

Early stage of *Suzy Wong's* reconstruction; Hamburg, New Jersey

Dan had copies of the original drawings from boat designer Sparkman & Stephens and intended to rebuild the *Suzy Wong* to those exact specifications. Naturally, he would make a few modern improvements because certain things available in 1959, when the boat was first built, were considered unusable today. Plans were laid for a stronger new engine, a better electrical system, and a more up-to-date galley.

Given the huge amount of time and effort that goes into restoring an old wooden boat, Dan's friends asked him why he didn't just build a brand-new boat. Dan's answer was always, "Because, it would be just another wooden boat." To Dan, it wasn't a matter of making it easy; it was far more important that his boat have a pedigree and a history. He wanted to take a famous boat—and the *Suzy Wong* was certainly that—and infuse new life into it that would carry it another thirty, forty, or fifty years.

What was intended as a three-year restoration project stretched to almost a decade. Dan and Emil worked two days a week, and sometimes three, on the restoration. They finished work on the hull, put in the bulkheads, re-planked the deck, and installed a new engine. The project then moved to some of the finer details of the restoration—like refinishing the hull and rigging the sails.

Beltram had set a deadline for himself. The boat had originally launched from Hong Kong in March 1960 and arrived in Miami by the end of July 1961. Beltram intended to re-launch the boat sometime in 2012, just after the fiftieth anniversary of the completion of *Suzy Wong*'s maiden voyage. His intention was that the original crew would be present to witness the re-launching and celebrate the continuation of the boat they had helped to build half a century earlier. But project deadlines have a way of being missed and, therefore, extended. Asked when his boat would be launched, Dan remarked, "I'm not going to predict launching dates anymore. It will happen when it happens!" Paul, Steve, George, and Walt plan to be there when it does, as long as they are, as Walt likes to say, "on the green side of the grass."

Chapter 56

THE WORLD OF SUZIE WONG
YEARS LATER

While the *Suzy Wong* will continue to sail on, *The World of Suzie Wong* (the story) is now largely forgotten. The novel by Richard Mason is largely forgotten too. Although it once was a bestseller, it has been out of print for many years. There are tattered used copies online, but there don't seem to be many takers for those.

The 1958 Broadway play was a modest hit, but it was very much a product of its era. It was never revived on Broadway. And it's unlikely that any school drama group would ever perform it because of the racy and adult subject matter. As far as the crew knows, no community-theater, summer stock, regional company, or dinner theater has paid royalties to perform the play in more than thirty years. It is an outdated stage relic.

The film premiered at Radio City Music Hall on Thanksgiving weekend in 1960. It became a sizable hit, one of the bigger box-office attractions of that next year, due mostly to the great chemistry between stars William Holden and Nancy Kwan. While female audiences enjoyed the glossy soap-opera plot, most critics (predominately male) complained about the film's sanitized depiction of prostitution. Obviously, those reviewers missed the point. *The World of Suzie Wong* was never meant to be an accurate portrayal of Hong Kong life; it was a Hollywood romance.

The film made Nancy Kwan a star, and she became the first Asian-American actress to play a leading role in a Hollywood movie. It also popularized the *cheongsam*, the high-collared form-fitting Chinese silk dress. In America the dress became an iconic fashion statement of the day, known as the Suzie Wong dress.

One of the film's most appealing qualities was its stunning location photography in Hong Kong. The crowds, colors, and sounds of Hong Kong created a rich reality. As movie studios were starting to cut back on production costs in the late 1950s, shooting on actual locations around the world was cheaper than building expensive outdoor sets, and soon this practice became more common. Instead of offering Hollywood's prettified view of the world, movies like *The World of Suzie Wong* opened audiences' eyes to exotic new worlds.

William Holden continued working for the next twenty years, appearing in twenty-six more films. He even received another Oscar nomination as Best Actor for *Network* (1976). He spent much of his later years as co-owner of the Mount Kenya Safari Club, dividing his time between Africa and Switzerland. Late in the night of November 16, 1981, a drunken Holden passed out, fell onto a glass coffee table, and gashed open his forehead. He bled to death on the living room carpet of his Hollywood apartment.

Publicist Irving Hoffman continued working right up until his death at age fifty-nine on December 9, 1968. His former roommate and fellow writer, Damon Runyon, wrote a tribute to Hoffman describing him as a "loose-jointed New York fellow, a man-about-tables, a squire of dames, a bon vivant, a raconteur. He should be one of the greatest writers of these times. He is a good caricaturist. A man can make a neat living with either accomplishment nowadays. Hoffman ignores them both in favor of press agentry. Maybe the mug fancies money. He is said to have some fat publicity accounts."

Like the book and the play before it, the movie *The World of Suzie Wong* is barely remembered these days. When someone does seek it out to watch on DVD or cable TV, it's usually because Holden's name, not Suzie Wong's, is drawing the interest.

CHAPTER 57

IN RETROSPECT

Steve, George, Walt, and Paul were between the ages of twenty-six and thirty-three when they journeyed by sea. The thought of building a boat and sailing it more than halfway around the world seemed like a good idea to them at the time. They were hardly fazed by the fact that they lacked any real sailing experience, and they could barely identify the basic parts of a boat. There were countless things they should have learned before embarking on this remarkable and dangerous voyage.

They disregarded good advice from seasoned sailors as to the wisdom of taking such a trip in the first place. After their voyage, one of the crew read a sailing book that highlighted five essential elements for a safe voyage: a good crew, lots of preparation, plenty of know-how, a good boat, and luck. Of those five elements, the *Suzy* crew had two—a proven ocean-going boat and amazing luck.

The *Suzy Wong* was a most forgiving lady; she handled well for the novice sailors. The difficulties they faced were the result of either their collective lack of experience or foolish mistakes, and their system of leadership was unorthodox. Onlookers probably thought the Americans looked ridiculous as they approached a pier or tried to catch a mooring buoy when the wind and currents disrupted what should have been an easy maneuver. They generally fared better on the open seas than they did nearer to land, but there was no one around to witness those triumphs.

Their dinghy was a joke. With everybody aboard, it sat just two inches above the waterline. The wake from any passing motorboat brought water pouring over the sides, sometimes swamping them. They nearly sank on more than one occasion. To get everyone ashore, they had to make multiple trips or try to convince a larger boat to ferry them. They nearly sank on more than one occasion.

Their electrical equipment consisted of a shortwave radio that enabled them to receive the essential time ticks for celestial navigation. GPS hadn't been invented, so they had to navigate by shooting the stars, often spending as long as two hours working on a star fix to calculate their position.

Cooking in their tiny galley, with an alcohol stove that had to be converted to kerosene, presented a daily challenge and some culinary disasters. However, they did enjoy reasonably good hot meals during the voyage, even on the roughest of seas. In fact, mealtimes were often the high point of each day.

They often worked their shifts in twosomes and they generally hung out that way when off duty as well. Walt and George had been stationed together during their naval careers; they shared a great interest in cars and liked going out to nice places for cocktails and dinner. Steve and Paul shared a more low-key manner, preferring to grab a quick bite and a beer before heading out to explore new destinations.

During their seventeen months together, the four men had their differences, and each had his idiosyncrasies. Walt could be bossy; Steve, impulsive; George was given to exaggeration; and Paul told jokes to the point of being a pain in the ass. Yet these personality quirks never became insurmountable problems. They knew they had to get along because their lives depended on it. As military men, they grasped that the group goal superseded the interests and desires of any individual. Each man respected the others (and himself) too much to engage in a temper tantrum that might have unnecessarily magnified a situation beyond its actual significance.

Many blue-water sailors don't make it past the first distant port. It takes unusually mature people to live together in such close proximity, and for such a prolonged duration. The *Suzy Wong* sailors were never more than an arm's length apart from each other for weeks on end, and they had no privacy. Adding to that, the nearly constant rolling and pitching of the boat could have easily contributed to a general mood of irritability. With all the challenges these novice sailors faced, it was a miracle that they were able to remain civil to one another and maintain reasonably good harmony throughout the voyage.

In all, they traveled roughly 26,000 miles from Hong Kong to Miami. This is only an estimate. There was no way of accurately counting the miles they logged traversing bodies of water such as the Indian Ocean, or the miles they tacked up the Red Sea. They estimated that their average speed was two miles per hour. Imagine going on a 26,000-mile trip averaging just two miles an hour! In the fifty years since the completion of the *Suzy Wong*'s maiden voyage, the world has become a far different place. It is certainly more dangerous and faster-paced. It would be almost impossible for Steve, George, Walt, and Paul to embark upon the same voyage today following the same course and under the conditions they faced all those years ago. In fact, our modern world is so accustomed to quick international travel that it's hard to imagine anyone having the patience to set out on a journey that would take seventeen months.

Yet, in the face of all the odds, these four young men had become the leading characters in their own epic saga—a story of heroic achievements. Even now, the cracks and crevices of time and age have not diminished the sailors' fond memories of the adventure that shaped their lives.

Estimable crew of the *Suzy Wong*: Steve, Paul, Gou, Walt, and George;
Junk Bay, Hong Kong

ABOUT THE BOOK

In October of 2009, the four sailors—Paul Cardoza, Steve Jackson, George Todd, and Walter Banks—reunited in Seattle, all together again for the first time in fifty years. While there, they viewed Paul's written memoir of their trip. It was then that the decision was made to write a book about their experiences together.

The road traveled toward the fruition of this book has taken longer than the voyage itself, but it has been just as exciting. Jonathan Lewis is credited with taking the interviews, news articles, letters, Paul's memoir, and Steve's drafts, and weaving them into a publishable work.

Looking back, it's fascinating to contemplate how these four individuals, previously strangers to each other, actually pulled off such an ambitious voyage. Yes, they had plenty of luck, but they undeniably proved they had the combined skills to successfully complete their remarkable venture.

Please visit our website for color photos, trailers, and contact information:

www.voyageofthesuzywong.com.

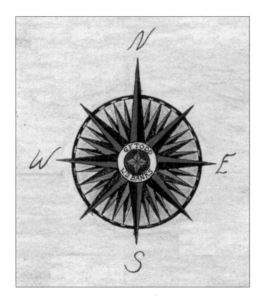

ABOUT THE SAILORS

PAUL CARDOZA was the character on the boat and its chief public relations director. He was quick-witted and could charm anyone with his card tricks and a knowing smile. He kept a storehouse of jokes for all situations, which he used to win over anyone within earshot. One such person he charmed was Irving Hoffman, the world-famous publicist who worked out a contract for the sailors with Paramount Pictures to promote the movie *The World of Suzie Wong*. This gave the crew an entry with generals, ambassadors, and monarchs and led to more than a few celebratory parties. Paul was also the one responsible for provisioning the food. There was never a day, despite the weather, when the crew didn't have a satisfying hot meal.

STEVE JACKSON was the youngest crew member. He brought a robust willingness to work hard. He was a jack-of-all-trades kind of guy and busied himself with any task needing to be done, both during the construction of the boat and when the adventure was underway. He was able to master the art of sailing and keep the sails and rigging in good working order. Steve had a yen for adventure. Without hesitation, he jumped at George's idea for the voyage at its conception and pressed forward to make the adventure come to life.

GEORGE TODD was the dreamer of the crew. It was, after all, his idea to initiate the trip. He was a good organizer, and there was plenty to organize for a global voyage. He was also the crew member who identified the boatyard, American Marine Limited in Hong Kong, and set in motion the

actual construction of the boat. Most of the early decisions fell on his shoulders. George was good looking, charming, and convincing, and he had a way about him that made it easy for key individuals to lend him a hand or, more importantly, a favor.

WALTER BANKS filled the crucial role of engineer and navigator. He was the cool head in situations that could have spelled disaster for the expedition. With his technical and naval navigational expertise, he was able to plot a safe course for the voyage

around the world. Walter didn't enter into frivolous conversation. In fact, he didn't say much at all. But when he did have something to say, it was important and everyone listened.

About Jonathan Lewis
Co-Author

"It is good to have an end to journey toward;
but it is the journey that matters, in the end."
~Ernest Hemingway

For Jonathan Lewis, all of his life has been a wonderful journey of shaping his artistic interests. From childhood he became a stage actor, a twenty-five year career that fostered an interest in literary structure and inspired him to do his own writing. In 1995 he became a travel writer for an adventure travel company, researching and writing about destinations all over the world, a career he continues to this day. For fourteen years he was a columnist for a Chicago magazine, eventually becoming the publication's editor. He has written on topics as diverse as film, history, and travel—all of which led him to the story of the *Voyage of the Suzy Wong*. He has traveled extensively to Asia, Africa, Europe, and Central America, and he makes his home in Chicago.

Remembering Paul Cardoza

Sadly, Paul Cardoza did not live to see the re-launching of the *Suzy Wong* or the publication of the book he initiated in 2009. His sons, John and Tony Cardoza, attended him in his final weeks. Together, they reread the manuscript, which gave him much pleasure. Paul was never one to pass up an opportunity to be a part of the action. He led a life of daring and adventure. His crewmates and family will miss his radiant personality along with his constant stream of stories, jokes, and magic tricks that gladdened the hearts of those around him.

A Final Note

As managing author of this book, Steve Jackson has had to respond to questions about himself and the *Suzy Wong*. One question asked was: "Looking back, what did you learn as a result of your voyage?" Steve responded that he came away from the trip realizing that people around the world are much the same, regardless of any outward appearance. They all love their families and enjoy a good joke or story. Steve also saw poverty and felt the many injustices in the world. It was mostly these experiences that led him to a career of service in the nonprofit world.

Another question asked of him was: "What advice would you offer to someone planning a similar adventure today?" Steve's answer: Dig deep into your innermost self and, like a miner searching for a treasure, find your passion, or the thing you love doing the most. Once you think you have found it, don't be afraid to take action—and don't be afraid of making a mistake. You never want to look back on your life with the regret that you failed to take advantage of an opportunity for fear of failure.

Steve was asked: "With four guys together on a small boat for such a long time, how well did you get along?" He replied that the four of them got along amazingly well, especially since they hadn't known each other at the outset. "We were lucky, of course, but basically we depended on each other to fulfill a needed and complementary team effort."

Finally, he was asked: "Do you have any comment about the re-launching of the boat this spring?" Steve answered that he wanted to wish "fair winds and good fortune" to Dan Beltram and his family, and to all who sail on Miss *Suzy Wong*.